My Love Affair With Italy

Memoir of a single woman's travels to Italy spanning 45 years from a teenager to retirement

Debbie Mancuso

donation

new Bok

#

Published by: A Passion for Italy, Lyndhurst, NJ
www.Facebook.com/MyLoveAffairWithItaly

Books may be purchased by contacting the publisher and author at:
dmancuso310@gmail.com

ISBN: 978-0-9989732-3-4
10 9 8 7 6 5 4 3 2 1
First Edition
Printed in the United States

In honor of the heroic and selfless acts of the 416,800 Americans, the 45,300 Canadians, and the 382,700 English men and women of the Allied Forces who gave their lives to liberate Europe in WWII, I dedicate this book.

Open my heart and you will see Graved inside of it, "Italy."

- Robert Browning

Preface

My passion for Italy started well before my first visit as a teenager. I never got tired of telling my stories, and people never seemed to get tired of hearing them. So, upon retirement, I put passion to paper.

As a single woman traveling alone most of the time, the experiences were unique beginning with the very first trip, and instead of fulfilling a dream of visiting the birthplace of all my ancestors, it only fueled what would become a life-long passion. Over the next 45 years, Italy would call me back 11 more times where I'd stay in farm houses, monasteries, a 1,000 year-old converted wine cellar in a medieval village, riding academies, a converted barn, Roman apartments, and magnificent vineyards. As an adult, I lived with another family while attending school and also shared an apartment with other students in Siena, all the while enduring extreme hardships at home. There would be emotional meetings as a result of finding family in the most unusual ways in remote villages of Italy 100 years later to the cave homes deep in the mountains of Sicily to its glorious shores.

It wasn't until I met a Roman that I found the "real" Rome outside of the main attractions, the jewels not mentioned in the brochures that take your breath away, the piazzas overflowing with life, and the people and the wine that make this country the second most visited place in the world.

Writing this book has only reinforced my love for Italy with its stunning vistas, incredible wines, warm and boisterous people, its art, its glorious history, warm and inviting waters, beautiful weather, and, of course, the amazing food.

Italy has always been a source of respite for me, a place to heal and reenergize, and even a place to date new and handsome Italian men, a country of many.   Hear how friendships made as a teen are rekindled four decades later with very surprising outcomes.

Acknowledgements

THANKS ARE DUE to Rita Chraim for her help and support, and to Robyn Monaco for her excellent advice.

To Christine Velezis, my Alabama Angel, for transforming this book from a travelogue to a memoir. A complete stranger, she appeared by chance on a hilltop in Tuscany the very next day after the first draft was completed. Her help and advice have been invaluable. A coincidence, I think not!

To Debbie Morrone-Afflitto and Jeanne Angela who have walked this path called life with me for the past 50 years, their love and support in good times and bad, in health and sickness have carried me through the most difficult days. I am forever indebted.

Each one has been heaven sent! This I know.

Introduction

I don't believe in coincidences. I prefer not playing cards and I avoid initiating conversation with strangers. The last being very uncharacteristic of my southern upbringing. That was prior to a fateful trip in 2015. Dear friends, the best kind, invited my husband, Michael, and I to join them on a trip to Italy. Not one to miss a travel adventure and a firm believer in the ethos that experiences are greater when shared, we accepted. We explored the lacework of canals, aging piazzas and the gilded domes of Venice. Afterwards, taking a train to Florence then navigating our way to a small-secluded winery and villa experiencing Tuscany's essence in the waning days of fall. For centuries the seduction of Italy constantly brings people back, us included.

We believed we were the only guests in this treasured jewel, nestled in a Tuscan hillside sheltered in a world of its own, a brief respite from the modern world. Although never eerie, the quietness, the unspoiled backdrop of rolling hills running throughout offered solitude, which could be heaven or hell depending on your outlook. Just land, just grape vines, just sky resplendent in the richest purple-orange hues, and just old friends. A strong and immediate connection could be felt with the land and only the stars, free from the tangle of buildings and lights, shinning a hushed silence, reverberating in the valley. People's stories are here. Last breaths and first cries are encased in the hallowed walls. For a brief moment we were part of its fabric. At that moment I was living the present, honoring the past and not looking beyond.

Taking a cue from our friend's natural sunny disposition to engage in conversations with complete strangers, I introduced myself while gingerly passing our neighbors' open window. Without prying I invited our neighbors to join us on the communal patio, unsure of their plans. After a few pleasantries exchanged, I am Southern born and Southern bred after all, I learned not only were our neighbors fellow Americans, but northeasterners. Although I could not feel the proverbial silent gasps when stating I, too, was American hailing from the south, I figured that would be the last I saw of them, except for brief exchanges in passing over the next few days.

Our friends were delighted when the formidable villa owner supplied us with a deck of playing cards. Not necessarily a good sign in my mind and definitely not my idea of how I was going to spend my nights in Italy. Sure, copious amounts of wine would flow and cheerful, boisterous conversations would be had. The odds were not in my favor of escaping from playing cards. I kept my opinions unspoken and acquiesced agreeing to play one hand, so the story goes. After the gentle pour of another rich wine, we noticed a handsome gentleman, our neighbor, donning a beret approaching our table. Immediately we extended him an invitation to join us, but first he had to answer an unsavory question, some issue we were presently debating. The four of us are a friendly bunch and welcome you by fire. Your facial gesture is typically your answer. Not batting an eye, he answered and returned the favor. We dealt him a hand. His fiancé, Debbie, joined us a short time later, after similar initiation. Fiery spirited and fiercely independent, she held her own. Unknowingly time progressed, sun setting on the naked vines and fog rolling in, casting a cool chill. Dew beset the blades of grass in the predawn hours eventually evaporating from the vines, while the vast region presented an inspiring palette. None of life's interruptions disrupted us. Engaging conversations and real face time, a lost art, was had. Intoxicating banter, energetic debates and friendly storytelling continued each evening.

Whether running to or from something, there is always a story. Everyone had their reasons for being there. A recent retiree, Debbie was there to write and simply revel in all of Italy's offerings. Ours was a shared desire to reconnect and quench our insatiable curiosity of the world around us. That nightly card table, peppered with deep knots and scared from heavy plates and wine glasses, and Debbie's ease, our common interests, and differing humor led to peculiar and stimulating discussions covering the realm of world politics to generational music to strong-willed opinions of religion. But just as pleasurable as the food and wine were, it was the union of six people gathered around a table where the world was discussed. No pretentions and no need to impress each other. It can take a lifetime, if ever, to have many of these in-depth conversations with some, never with Debbie. Our differences didn't divide us. Debbie and I had just as many similarities. Perhaps an unconventional pair, our age gap, life roles and career choices didn't matter. Today's conversation became tomorrow's favorite memory, those frequently and fondly recalled.

Not granted more time, the magic ended. We bid our farewells exchanging emails, an uncommon gesture on my part. We returned to the heart of the Tuscan region, Florence, for a few days before heading home. Debbie migrated south to electric filled, high energy, yet sometimes fragile, Rome, another great love of hers. It was a glorious end to yet another once in a lifetime experience: the food, the wine, the history and the relationship with others, the simplest blueprint for a fulfilling life.   Along the way you gather, lose, sometimes find again and even prune people in your life.   Although a brief encounter, Debbie will be a friend I cherish.

Anyone who has attempted to formulate their stories quickly realizes how daunting a blank page can be, even lonely at times.   With time and patience the process, sometimes painstakingly slow, evolves into a final project, one of passion. Debbie's passion blurs the lines from work to pleasure. I encourage you to approach her stories engaging all senses with an understanding that you see not only with your eyes, hear not only with your ears and feel not only with your hands, instead sometimes with your soul, heart and even your head. Debbie confirms that we all want, not just Italian descendants, the same things: health of family and friends, faith and good food.   While Sinatra plays, I can smell the aroma from her kitchen and almost taste her homemade ravioli and gravy simmering and wine poured, a true Italian with no recipe, but a technique with a "feel" and secret pan.   I hope I am one of the fortunate ones she imparts her ravioli wisdom to with patience and guidance.

Italy's allure continually beckoned her.   She crafted her lifetime love of travel coupled with the loves of her life at various stages, the devotion and duty to family, childhood friends and even an unlikely fiancé. Everyone has a story. Debbie, a resilient soul and a tough cookie, takes you on those lifetime of stories with sojourns abroad, what was gained and lost, while always remaining in the present.   Just as Italy has done for thousands of years, Debbie persevered, adapting to various roles, playing the hands that were dealt. From teenage angst, to marriage, through divorce, caretaker for a dying parent, the good, the bad, and the complexities of life in between. I respect Debbie's commitment to write in her voice and, more importantly, her honesty and always with sincerity. I love hearing peoples' stories especially as our memoires begin to fade and finally erase. She inspires all to put pen to paper with stories that connect or reconnect us to people and places and the things we have learned along the way.

A Southern and a New Jersey native walk into a small winery. That could be the start of any corny joke, but instead it was the beginning of a sincere friendship, something where nothing was expected, but everything was gained.

-Christine

Table of Contents

Chapter One

Life at Home: 1970

My name is Debbie, or Deborah if Mom is really mad. I'm finishing the last week of my junior year in high school, and I live with my parents, Betty and Ray, and my two younger sisters, Nicey, age fifteen, and "The Baby," age seven, in a small town in New Jersey just ten miles from New York City. I'm turning seventeen in three days, and three days after that, I am leaving for a student tour of Italy, France, and Switzerland. I don't know anyone going; it's a trip I've heard about from my Italian teacher. He always wanted one of his students to take his course seriously, and now I'm actually going to his homeland and the homeland of all my ancestors, Italy. It wasn't without great effort, however, on my part. After all, my dad isn't the type to pay for anything like this, and I've never been away from home without a parent in my life. I've never even been on an airplane.

I have this draw to Italy, and I don't know how it all started. I'm full-blooded Italian like so many of the kids I go to school with. My mom's parents were born in the United States, and no one in her family ever spoke about even wanting to visit Italy. My dad's parents, whom I didn't know and were both born in Sicily, left their homeland when they were young children, barely old enough to remember it. Yet, for some reason I have this draw to there, so much so that I've relentlessly battered my parents until they agree to send me.

I am leaving everyone behind for 40 days. I never dreamed of asking Dad for this much money, and I don't want to take advantage of his generosity, so I took a job after school

1

at a commercial bakery boxing pies with one of my best friends, Jeanne, for the spending money I'll need. Mom and I are always arguing over their favoritism to one of my sisters, and I want to be away from all the fighting. I never know when she and I will go off like a rocket. Very loud is the only volume we use when speaking to each other. The anger is palpable.

Dad is a nice looking, middle-aged man who is self employed. He and his family have always owned grocery stores. Not the size of the new large ones being built, but one of those friendly, independent stores where most people purchase their perishables. Dad's store sells fresh fish, produce, and canned goods, and he knows nearly every one of his customers by their first names, including the babies whom he favors. The store is in a lower to lower-middle-class neighborhood of many nationalities, and so many of his customers purchase on credit. I don't mean credit cards; I mean Dad himself extends them credit. He simply writes in his black ledger book what the new purchases are, adds it to their existing balance, and the customers pay when they can. That is the only record he keeps of his receivables. Dad is a very easy going, affable guy with a dry sense of humor that everyone seems to love. On his way home, he even delivers food orders to the customers who cannot get to the store. I don't think my father ever had an enemy in his life. In addition to selling fish and groceries, Dad is also a bookie. Not a big time bookie like we're accustomed to seeing on television, but merely a numbers' bookie. The only gambling he takes is on three numbers coming out either straight or in a combination, a box. It's only three numbers, and no one becomes millionaires overnight. Dad receives 25 percent commission when someone hits, plus they always give him a tip. It's easy money for the most part, but it has a big downside – it's illegal. We've learned as children growing up

2

to never speak of it out of the family – ever. None of my friends or boyfriends know; it's no one's business. Dad got into booking numbers accidentally. The man who actually takes the action, the top boss, is a childhood friend of his, but not a close one. Other than this connection, there is no other contact between us and families of organized crime. Dad calls the numbers in over the phone under the name "Bing," a nickname given to him as a young man because he sang just like Bing Crosby. On Sundays, Dad delivers the money to the "boss" who lives in the next town, and occasionally I'll even make the drop for Dad. I'll do it for my father, but I don't like it even though the boss is very nice to me. Other than the numbers, I don't think Dad has any knowledge of any additional unlawful activity of his, but I am more than intimidated. He lives in a somewhat modest home, but it's the German Shepherds I need to pass that scare the crap out of me. I say my polite hello's, make the drop quickly, and fly off in the new Dodge Charger I share with Mom. Fortunately, Dad has never gotten into any trouble as a result of booking numbers; he gives gifts of cash to the cops at Christmastime that look away. There's no pressure; it's always friendly. They, too, like Dad.

The second income affords us a nice life. Not extravagant in any way, but my dad is capable of giving us one of the nicest homes in town and nice cars. As a young child, we had a summer home and even a "Sunday" car. It was one of those automobiles with great big fins. The fins were so big and scary that Mom would never back it out of the garage. We'd wait for Sunday when Dad was home.

Even though Dad is booking numbers, it's a business to him. It's Mom who is the real gambler, and it often becomes a problem. She has access to the numbers being called in every Wednesday and Friday when she works for Dad at the fish store, and she adds her own bets without him knowing. Mom

3

doesn't get paid for the days she works; he is giving her a set allowance every week, which is never enough according to her. It was a long time before I realized that the real problem with her lack of funds had to do with her gambling. I'd hear her on the phone telling someone how much money she lost in the card game the night before – the **weekly** card game held in our home. I didn't understand as a little kid why I couldn't be a Brownie because the uniform was expensive when I knew we had two homes, not to mention the other real estate Dad owned. And doesn't Aunt Massie always call him a millionaire? Truth is when he'd open his big safe in my parents' walk-in closet, he didn't keep cash in it, no jewelry, definitely not a gun. He kept his bag of Hershey Kisses locked up.

The best thing that came out of their gambling was the one hit Dad had for $2,500. With those winnings, he installed a built-in pool for us. We suddenly became even more popular. Mom buys whole sections of cows at a time and goes through it within weeks with all the family she's feeding in the summer. Our home is never empty; you never realize how many family and friends you have until you have a pool. Mom loves every minute of it and has no interest in vacationing anywhere else in the world. She wants to stay home, as I want to be on another continent.

Our home appears seemingly large, stately looking, set atop a small hill and made entirely of brick, something important to an Italian man. The Romans perfected brick-making thousands of years ago and taught the world. Our home is very ornate from the moment you walk through the door. Mom decorated it just like any respectable Italian-American: large statues dominate the living room and foyer, and the plastic covers protect the green velvet couch from ever being soiled. Once you pass through the foyer, you come to Dad's recliner where he sits from 6:45 pm to bedtime after his 12-hour workday. Our home is always busy and gets so much traffic that our carpeting is replaced every two years. Gangs of people pass Dad's recliner, and if he is awake, he just nods and says hi because he is too tired to say much more. The boyfriends don't realize why he is so short on language, and they are intimidated by the house alone. We look like people of some affluence, and we happen to be Italian. And Dad is not saying anything while checking them out as they pass by. Then they enter the kitchen and meet my mom. It's like they landed on another planet from one room to another. As quiet as Dad is, Mom is very vocal, warm, and extremely hospitable. She's a nice-looking, shapely, buxom, bleached blonde with a great big personality to match. She could actually pass for Mae West's younger sister and has the qualities to be dangerous! Mom makes everyone laugh from the moment they meet her, and she makes our home a favorite place for all our friends to meet. Her favorite word is fuck, and because of this, my best friends, Debbie, Jeanne, and Roberta, want to move in. Of my friends, I'm the most outgoing, the most gregarious; I can speak to anyone and not be shy. As free as my mom is with her language, she's very stern with us about sex. No sex before marriage - ever. I'm told if I ever come home pregnant, I'm disowned. I wouldn't dream of asking her a question about sex, she'd probably die, but ironically she can have a pretty dirty mouth, and occasionally she embarrasses me. She'd never speak like that around Dad. He won't tolerate the "F" word. I'm pretty sure she's using these offensive words around her mother, aunts, and cousins, and they always find it hysterical. But occasionally she slips around me, and, except for the word fuck, I never find it funny.

I started taking Italian classes freshman year. In the beginning, I'd come home, study the words, and practice them aloud.

Mom was very happy I was taking Italian and actually loved hearing me, even though she hadn't a clue if I was saying it correctly or not. She just boasted to the family about me learning to speak Italian. But whenever I'd try to speak it, Uncle Sal, who lives on the second floor and is the only one born in Sicily and speaks Italian, would discourage me so much because my pronunciation was never good enough. No Italian would understand a word I was saying, he made me feel. After a short time, that feeling drove me to stop practicing. Yet Mom would continue to tell people that I was almost fluent in Italian. My aunt and uncle would laugh knowing that wasn't nearly the truth, and Mom would honestly get upset with Uncle Sal for discouraging me. To her, I am nearly fluent. I think she's nuts, but I do like the encouragement she is giving me.

I am very fortunate to have the great deal of freedom Mom affords me. She was raised by an abusive, alcoholic father who gave her no freedom. He was so mean that Grandma cried when they released her from the hospital. She didn't want to go home. When Mom was pregnant with her first child, Grandpa got mad at her and wished her baby to die. The baby girl was dead at birth. Life was hell for my grandmother and her three daughters; they all suffered his abuse until the day they married. Mom promised our lives would never resemble hers, and, as a result, raises us completely the opposite. I have all the freedom I want, within reason, up until to the point I'm found lying. But I never have to. You can say my mom gave me my first set of wings, Dad financed them, and someone I'd meet soon in Italy would teach me how to use them.

The night of my 17th birthday, a big party is planned in our finished basement. One of my classmates offered to have his band play, so we set up the attached double garage for the band and dancing. Mom ordered a great birthday cake shaped into an airplane and adorned with the American flag. It would be only weeks later I'd get to understand the real symbolism of that flag. The house is overflowing with kids I've never met before, and the party is quickly becoming a huge success. Mom has never sent her kids away other than to family, so this is a big deal for her, too. We'll all have a reprieve from the bickering and yelling, and Mom can have that quiet summer in her backyard entertaining family by the new pool. I'll be thousands of miles away – so she thinks.

My three best friends will accompany Mom to the airport. Mom has a wedding the same day I leave for Rome, and one of my sisters, a/k/a Mom's favorite, is in the wedding party. Mom can't be in two places at the same time, so guess who gets bumped? She gets the idea from someone to drop me off at Newark International Airport to catch a helicopter over to JFK Airport to meet my plane. All of a sudden we are the Rockefellers. Are you kidding me? Would she actually drop me off at a different airport in a different state to catch a helicopter to the plane? The "special one" has a wedding that day, and Mom doesn't want to miss her walking down the aisle, so she'll drop me off at the closest heliport? Would she really do this? .... OF COURSE, she will.

After a while when the idea of the helicopter settles with me, I'm okay with it. I have visions of flying in a helicopter, just me and the pilot.

The four of them walk me to the gate where we all embrace and say our good-byes. I am going to really miss my friends; there wasn't anything we did apart for the past five years, and now I'm leaving for the entire summer. We drive around the hot spots and cruise the avenue all night on two dollars of gas when we aren't with our steady boyfriends and their friends. My steady is Richie, and we've been together for over a year. Summer won't be the same without the blue Charger and all of us together. As I reach the gate waiting to board the helicopter and begin my new adventure, I embrace everyone again, and we all start crying, especially Mom. I am crying from the anxiety of going it alone, but why is Mom crying? Isn't this what she wants? I know she loves me, but I think she'll remember that more if I leave for some time.

I'm escorted to the helicopter, and to my real surprise, it's quite different than I ever imagined. It's much larger than the ones the weather guy reports from, and we're not alone. There are about 10 other people flying with me, seemingly all business professionals. There's even a stewardess. I can't believe there are enough people who actually take helicopters that they even need a stewardess!

The engine starts, and the loud, swishing sound of the helicopter's blades is both frightening and exciting. The feeling of ascending straight up feels more like an amusement ride than a mode of transportation. I haven't flown in an airplane before, but I know this is amazing! We arrive at our second stop, JFK Airport, and I'm let out. Mom didn't think to ask if they'd drop me off at the terminal the plane was departing from, and when we land, I'm informed I have to go to a different terminal. Already thrown for a loop, it never occurs to me to ask for a taxi. Instead, I inch my way to the other terminal by pulling two pieces of luggage at a time and then stopping and going back for the other two pieces. It's June 20th, and it's really hot under the blazing sun. This is already not going well.

In between terminals, there's an island that divides the road. I'm standing on the island with two elderly women waiting for the light to turn green, and I see from a distance a military bus approaching. As the bus gets closer, I hear the screams of the men who are standing with their hands raised in excitement from their bus' windows. Not giving it much thought, I assume they are listening to a Yankee game. I watch the bus as it passes me by, and I'm anxious to get on with my own journey. When it passes, the woman next to me turns to me and says, "You know that was for you, don't you?" I reply, "No, I thought it was for Thurman Munson." I'm blown away. I realize these men are probably coming home from serving a tour of duty in Vietnam and haven't seen a young American girl in at least a year. This explains their enthusiasm.

I arrive at the correct terminal just in time where my Italian language professor, Mr. Zappola, is happy to see me. I cut it so close that he doesn't even have time to introduce me to anyone in my group.

***

Exhausted after the long flight, we navigate our way through historic Rome.   Driving past the Coliseum and Circus Maximus on the way to our "hotel" takes my breath away. I recognize all of it, having seen pictures of them hundreds of times when Dad was watching his old, epic movies like Ben Hur, volume on high and Mom screaming in the background, "Ray, Ray, lower that damn television. It sounds like they're racing in our living room." We all have a big laugh. The Coliseum always amazed me, but nothing could have prepared me for how I feel when I see it for the very first time. I can visualize the nearly 100,000 screaming people inside and the roar of the lions as they go against the gladiators. More than 60 percent of the Coliseum still stands nearly 2,000 years later, and I'm living only two blocks away from it for the next several weeks. Dad won't believe it!

Our accommodations are atop one of Rome's seven hills, Caelian Hill, located in front of the Palatine. The antique white building is three stories high and has a church on the grounds that's linked by a beautiful courtyard. The church, San Gregorio, had its beginning as a simple oratory added to a family villa of Pope Gregory I who converted the villa into a monastery circa 575-80 before his election as Pope in 590. The trees surrounding the property add to its beauty, but more importantly, they provide much needed shade under Italy's blistering sun. There is a long, stone retainer wall about three feet high that hugs the building's property line and extends down the hill. It's just high enough to sit on comfortably without me needing help getting onto it. Yes, the accommodations don't look like any hotel I've ever seen, but what do I know about Italian hotels? I'm in Italy, and I don't care. It is a small hill, a very small hill, which means it is quick and easy to get to, and it's a mere two blocks from the Coliseum. I still can't believe it. Wait till I tell Dad!

10

The bus driver empties the luggage from the bottom of the bus, and we each grab our own to carry to our rooms. We enter the building through an old iron gate, through the double doors of the residence, through the foyer, and finally, the lobby. The lobby area has the typical Italian terra cotta flooring with high ceilings and a staircase at the far end that leads to the second floor where the bedrooms are located. No elevator. Just before the stairs, there is the one public telephone on the right wall that is used mostly for incoming calls. I won't understand the Italian operator, so there is no way I'll be using it. If the phone rings, I can say "Pronto," but that is as far as I'll get with a conversation.

After lugging all my suitcases up the stairs, I am given a very pleasant room facing the courtyard with two single beds on the opposite sides of the room. I quickly see that one of the most beautiful pleasures in Italy is opening the shutters for the very first time and taking in the view. It's like opening a gift Christmas morning, a total surprise. Their shutters are actually used for practical purposes like blocking the sun instead of blinds or drapes like us Americans. I feel like I'm in a movie. Because our bedroom is facing the courtyard, it is unusually quiet for this high-energy city. Pushing the shutters open and letting the light come through for the first time in the morning feels almost ceremonial. You welcome in the day and say good morning to God without even knowing it.

My roommate is a 20-year-old girl from Connecticut of Portuguese descent with long, straight dark hair. She is sweet looking, pleasant, quiet and makes for a great roommate. For adventure, there's someone else: Linda. Linda and I meet the very first day and become inseparable. She's petite with long, thick blonde hair, tiny figure, and she loves to dance. She's also extremely outgoing, rarely stops talking, and she immediately becomes my idol. She shares a room with three other students in our group at the end of the hall. Linda just completed her associate's degree in Waterbury, Connecticut, along with the rest of the students I'll be studying with every day from 8:30 am – 12:30 pm. All of them have had our Italian professor, Mr. Zappola. I'm the only outsider. I quickly discover that the touring company made a mistake and put me with college students, which means I won't be chaperoned! Once I complete this six-week course successfully, I'll receive three college credits. I really don't want to wake up and be in school at 8:30 a.m. during the summer *anywhere* in the world, but this is the only way I was getting here. After *mezzogiorno*, or noon, we are free to do what we wish – no chaperones! All I need to do is follow Linda who speaks a little Italian. The fact that we hit it off from the start and she took me under her wing makes it much easier and more fun for me. What a gift from heaven.

One of our first stops: The Trevi Fountain, the most famous and largest fountain in all of Rome, is actually the façade of a large palace. It's even more exquisite than I've seen in any photo or movie. But I'm taken by the actual small size of the piazza where it was built in 1735. Linda and I do the obligatory throwing of the coins in the fountain to ensure our return to Rome. And, of course, there has to be shopping, too. This piazza consists of all stores on the ground level with people cramming into this small space for the same ceremonial toss of coins and photo ops. It is terribly hot and uncomfortable as we're all packed into this diminutive space. Linda and I decide to separate and meet back at a designated time to shop. I buy new white leather shoes with a matching white brimmed hat and, of course, gelato. As I'm waiting for Linda, I sit down next to a gentleman and politely turn to him and say: *"scusami, signore, che ora e'?"* I'm proud of myself; I actually spoke Italian to someone for the first time out of class. It feels good. I wonder if he understands me and if I'll get a chance to say anything else? Just as I begin to feel more confident, he turns to me and says, "Why don't you just say "What time is it?""

Before leaving home, Mom kept telling me to call when I arrive and, of course, I tell her yes, the only answer a mom wants to hear. However, when we arrived, I quickly became aware that this was not going to be easy. Besides the fact that I won't understand one word an Italian operator is speaking, there is a phone strike, and there's no way I can call home. Mom can figure out that I'm fine. She'd certainly hear if there was a plane crash. I have so many other adjustments; I can't be bothered with going crazy about calling home. I'll write; she'll get it in about a week. She knows I'm not really afraid.

The following morning I ask where the showers are when I can't find one on our floor. This is not the United States, and I can't expect an en suite bathroom. I've never been to college, but this looks more like a dorm than a hotel to me. I'm told that the showers are on the next floor up. As I climb the stairs and enter the third floor restroom, I see that they are like college dorm showers where there is one room with many stalls. I can live with this. The toilets are all different and nothing like I've ever seen. Each time I walk into a building to use one, I never know how it is going to be constructed, how to flush it, or if I will have to pay to use it. They have pull chains or pedals to flush, and I'm told sometimes there's simply a hole in the ground. I've figured out how to flush the toilets here, so I'm sure I can conquer the shower as well. The only real surprise is the singing I hear from one of the stalls, and it doesn't sound like a woman at all. Fortunately, I save myself a great deal of potential embarrassment by speaking up and learning that the person in the next stall is, in fact, a man. I immediately think I'm in the men's showers until he advises me that the showers are coed. Wow, Italy is progressive! This is really uncomfortable for me, and I know with certainty that it would not be acceptable to Mom, but what can I do? I will leave out this one small detail when I speak of my trip to her. She'd be so pissed. But there is no harm done and nothing I can do about it either. Somehow, though, it would be my fault that there's a guy here.

Our Italian language group is small, less than 10 students between the guys and the girls. Waking up and sitting through four hours in class, I quickly realize this class is well over my head, it's no fun at all, and for the first time, I am severely behind the rest of my class. My Italian instructor at home has no command of his pupils, and instead of teaching us, he ends up attempting to discipline the students the entire period every single day. I've had two full years of the same behavior with the exact same results. I wanted to learn, but I couldn't, and he's the only Italian teacher we have. If I didn't learn, no one else did either.

Mr. Zappola is kind, but he doesn't know what to do with me. He's frustrated; I'm sure he doesn't want to fail anyone, especially having come this far, but I can't even remember how to say the name of the residence of where I'm living; it's much too long. I don't feel comfortable telling him the real reason I know so little. I sit through these agonizing classes in the beautiful courtyard that separates the "hotel" from the church, but at least I'm still with Linda. I think how I want to be back in bed like any normal teenager and then think how it could be worse.... I could be in regular summer school at home taking Italian. I'm so moved by the ambiance, I attend their mass on Sunday. There are only a few other people in attendance.

After a few days, I remark to Linda that there are quite a few priests around our "hotel" and how unusual I think it is. And what about the fact they have no reception desk; there's always one on television. My only past travel accommodations were booked with family. If Aunt Marie expects you and it's Saturday, then it's steak and thick French fries for dinner. I hate steak, and I hate those fries, but I'm always happy to see my aunt! She's one of my biggest fans. Then Linda stuns me when she says that we're actually living in a monastery and not a hotel. Are you kidding me? Our itinerary states a hotel, and I'm in a monastery? It's almost funny. After the initial shock, I realize it's not really a problem. Everyone treats us well, the location is fantastic, and the food is good. I'm pretty happy, no real change in plans, and Mom doesn't need to know - so I think. I'm doing well and living at San Gregorio's Monastery on one of the seven hills of Rome. Just don't ask me how to say it in Italian. Could life get any better for a 17-year-old kid? I don't think so.

Linda and I walk down to the Coliseum in the afternoons to check things out. It quickly becomes our hang-out; there's no better place in the world! There's a park between San Gregorio and the Coliseum which we quickly learn to cut through. Once we arrive at the Coliseum, we see all kinds of vendors selling their goods off small trucks or wagons. My absolute favorite is the gelato vendor. It's like your first kiss, you just don't ever forget it. Chocolate, of course. It's rich and creamy, but not like ice cream and has a texture somewhere between a lemon ice and American ice cream. I can't believe I've never tasted it in the United States. After all, everywhere I go at home there are Italians. What an extraordinary treat and in a hundred flavors, too. I only need chocolate.

Linda will talk to anyone who passes us, and she makes finding places and getting information easy. After she gets the information she needs, she dismisses the people who gave her the information just as easily. Once she gets what she wants, she has no need for them. While passing through the park to get to the Coliseum, we quickly notice men are appearing out of the dark from behind the trees. After the third guy appears, Linda and I take off like bats out of hell and take the long route. When we arrive, she tells the *carabinieri* of our experience, and the police explain that this park is inhabited with prostitutes and that is what they think we are. It also explains all the women dressed in skimpy clothing at the Coliseum. It's such a rude awakening when I learn that the Coliseum is now a house of ill repute. How did it ever drop that low? The neighborhood had certainly changed in the last 2,000 years. Not at all what I had expected of the glory of Rome. Or maybe it hadn't changed that much after all.

Our Italian group consists of both guys and girls, and some are pairing off already. They've formed cliques, too. Natural evolution at its best. I have a steady boyfriend at home, Richie, and I'm not looking for a fling in Italy; not even thinking about it...........yet. But one of the students from California, Jerry, a struggling actor, has his eyes set on me. At first, I just thought he was friendly, but Linda could tell that he was interested in more than a friendship with me. I never liked dating strangers, mostly out of fear, so my dating pool consisted of guys from my hometown or very near. Richie is a great boyfriend; many would say perfect. He's the kind of kid you'd see on a television soap opera: handsome, sweet, Italian, plays guitar professionally and sings well, too. But most of all he adores me. Mom loves Richie, and both families are marrying us off already in their heads before I even turn 17! But I don't want to go there; I don't love him that way. If I cheat or leave Richie, he'll be devastated, and this will cause a problem between Mom and me. Richie is truly a good guy from a good family, but I just don't want to get engaged to <u>anyone</u> in the near future. I've been fortunate enough to date some very nice and very cute boys, and now my mom wants me to stop!

Am I willing to betray Richie? Well,.......... maybe. But not so easily. Jerry makes every attempt to get my attention beyond a polite conversation, and to no avail. But, soon after, my thoughts start to go to him, and foolish me didn't even realize that he had already moved on after all my rejections. He's dating one of the plain girls and formed their own clique. I miss out because I waited too long. When I realize that I had been replaced, I am heartbroken. I started to care for him and his attention more than I realized, even the way he teases me, especially when he always calls me Miss New Joysie. A different outcome would have given me the kisses, the hugs, and a romantic Roman holiday in this magnificent city. I'd miss out on it all. Instead, I've come to learn what it feels like to miss him, and he's so close.

One night Linda befriends a young Italian man, and we're asked to go for a drive. By now, I trust Linda's judgment without question, maybe stupidly so, and a bunch of us from class pack into her new friend's car and go for a drive on the Appian Way, one of Rome's oldest and most historic roads built in 312 BC. The weather is incredibly beautiful as we drive down this majestic *strada* flanked by high pine trees and cypresses. While Via Appia is lined with monuments and tombs of ancient Roman patrician families, many find what's under the Appian Way to be more interesting. Below the street are miles of tunnels, catacombs, where the early Christians buried their dead and, when necessary, held secret church services. We stop at a café for drinks under the Italian moonlight. As I sit next to the handsome Italian who drove us here, I realize he is interested in me and not Linda. Then he goes to his trunk and pulls out a guitar and starts to sing. Of all the talents he could possess, it's guitar playing and singing just like Richie! To me, it's the same act, just on a different continent.

Being here, sipping wine alfresco in one of the most historic places on earth, feels like a glance into heaven. I get another chance to spend time with this handsome Italian the following day when he takes me to his father's clothing store in Rome to meet his parents. He's very nice, but he's not Jerry, and I won't be staying in Rome much longer anyway.

All meals are included in our trip and provided by the monastery. The dining room isn't old; it's ancient, 1,395 years old to be specific. It has plain, white, cracked, dull walls with old, worn paintings hanging, some of them even torn, but the food is perfectly sufficient and enjoyable. I haven't had any of those meals like Mom's roast beef. She has perfected the dish so perfectly, I swear I can hear the cow mooing. The tables are set up in long rows, and except for the linen tablecloths and people serving us our meals, the room feels like it's a step up from a cafeteria. They serve pasta every night to start, and unlike the macaroni and meatballs at home, they serve an outstanding meat sauce called Bolognese that I need to tell Mom about. But I have two problems: first, they only serve espresso, wine, or water with our meals, and then there is the napkin situation. You wouldn't think that napkins could in any way be a real problem, but this took me aback: We are given a linen napkin when we arrive for our first meal that's placed in a leather folder with our name on it. Why the folder and why our names on them? Because the napkins are washed only once a week! By the end of the week, you'd prefer to use your sleeve to wipe your face than your own napkin. This gives new meaning to recycling. Didn't they ever hear of paper? The drinking situation presents a bigger problem because I never drink espresso, wine, water, or any coffee.

Dad brings home a large bottle of Coca-Cola every night from the store. The monastery has a vending machine full of soft drinks, including Coca-Cola, but the problem is the quantity of coins it takes for just one bottle. Enough to fill a change purse. Most days I manage to have the right amount, but other days I fall short and drink wine. It doesn't take long before I'm feeling a little tipsy, and the "guardians" notice. They realize, too, that the travel company made a mistake with my age, yet never attempted to do anything about it. But I can tell they are concerned, especially when I drink the wine.

As is typical of monasteries in Italy, they lock their doors at 11 p.m. If you aren't in by 11, you're homeless for the night. Linda befriended a young student, Cesare, who is living in the monastery while attending medical school in Rome. Cesare is a somewhat quiet guy from the South of Italy, like you would imagine a medical student to be, and enjoys the company of the female American students. He's friendly with us all. He seems shy, but maybe he's shy to speak English. But I understand him very well. We speak often, and I always feel he is interested in Linda. I think everyone is interested in her. Cesare is also kind and friendly and often joins our group when we venture out. But our favorite show of kindness from him is how he waits for us at night and opens the gate for Linda and me when we arrive after 11. As it turns out, I don't have a chaperone or have a curfew thanks to Cesare.

Many of the evenings are spent in the monastery dining room after we return from the Coliseum, or anywhere else Linda and I wander before heading back for the night. We push the tables and chairs to the side of the room and play the radio. It doesn't matter if the songs are Italian or English; we'll dance to either. Even the workers at the monastery join in. Our favorite song this summer is Italy's favorite song: Lady Barbara. It doesn't matter that I don't understand one word; we jump to dance every time.

19

Linda enjoys sun bathing, and she talks me into sunning on the terrace. That evening, our counselor approaches us to say that we are kindly asked by the monastery to stop sunbathing on the property. We are too much of a distraction to the monks!

We have an excursion away from the monastery for a few days down in the South of Italy to visit Sorrento, Capri, and Pompeii. We arrive in Sorrento in our large bus, and as we pass along the busy, narrow streets lined with lemon and orange trees, we can actually pick the enormous fruit from the bus' windows. The entire landscape is dotted with them. The lemons are the size of oranges, and the oranges are the size of grapefruits. They are growing all over the place, and the hot Italian sun blesses them in abundance.

We actually have a real hotel in Sorrento where we can swim without disturbing any monks. From Sorrento, we are bused to the busy port of Naples where we'll take a ferry boat to the island of Capri for the day. Upon arrival onto Capri, we take a bus to the top of the island called Ana Capri. We continue to climb on foot by ascending the stairs to the beautiful row of small shops where I purchase a green bikini (I am getting into the when-in-Rome thing and ditched the modest one piece). After making several purchases, I notice a cable car ride almost immediately next to this plateau. I pay my lire and hop onto the car to begin my climb to the summit. The ride is simply stunning. The cable car takes you up and down the side of the mountain where we are a mere feet away from being able to touch the landowners' trees. A few more feet and we'll be able to pick the fruit right from the cable car.

As we glide past their homes and gardens, I can overhear the conversations. It feels almost intrusive. Even though I don't understand a word, what touches me is the laughter I hear between the moms and the kids. I can only think of my mom and how I missed her laughter and how I've taken it for granted. The laughter sounds like music now. When I reach the summit, I take in the 360 degree view of the island overlooking the bluest of Mediterranean waters below. The return ride is just as glorious.

Once we are done touring Sorrento, we are escorted to a small boat which will take us around the island. The boats are small and can only accommodate half our group, and two boats go out simultaneously. Linda and I remain together along with the rest of the ladies in our Italian class, but Jerry is in the other boat with his new clique. It's painful watching him with someone else knowing it should have been me, how badly I messed this once-in-a-lifetime romance up. When the boats drop their anchors and cut their engines, we are free to jump off and swim. My parents had owned two summer homes on the Jersey shore, so I am accustomed to swimming in an ocean, but no Jersey coastline comes close to this. As we ride above the sea, the color of the water changes from vibrant blue to turbid green as if God himself colored it with a crayon and didn't feel like staying within any lines. And unlike the Jersey shore, the water is incredibly warm. There is no getting your toes wet first and inching your way into the ocean. Here I can just dive in and feel the sensation of the warm water bathe every inch of my body. The richest kids in the world have nothing on me today; I'm playing on the Mediterranean. Except for the failed romance with Jerry, life can't get any better than today.

The following day we are escorted to Pompeii and walk through the ruins under the blistering Italian sun. There's no escaping it, no shade to give us some reprieve, just the scorching hot sun. After hearing the history of this place, I become intrigued. I'm especially struck by how the people were entombed after the quake that destroyed the entire city and remained covered until the first excavation began in1748. It is written that on August 20, 79 AD, the earth began to rumble and crack, and the usually calm sea gave way to giant waves. Horses, cattle and birds became uneasy and restless, as if they could foresee the disaster that awaited the town. Finally, on the morning of August 24th, the volcano burst open with an earsplitting crack. Smoke, mud, flames and burning stones spewed from the summit of the mountain, sending a rain of ash and rock through the surrounding countryside. The mud seeped down the sides of Vesuvius, swallowing nearby farms, orchards and villas. Adding to the destruction were the mephitic vapors that accompanied the falling debris; the fumes first caused deliriousness in their victims, then suffocated them. Its inhabitants who could not escape were killed by falling buildings, overcome by the mephitic gas, or simply buried by the rapidly falling ash. Their bodies were quickly covered by the volcano's mineral deposits, which covered Pompeii in a layer more than 30 feet thick!

Many weren't just lying there like you'd expect to see a dead body. They had their arms extended as if trying to protect themselves from an attacker, and many had their children beneath their own bodies in an effort to protect them. It would be many hundreds of years before they would be excavated for everyone to see how this world was destroyed and how these people lived. Because of the writings on the walls, archeologists now know exactly what kind of businesses they had, what they ate, how their homes were, and how they entertained themselves. It was a smaller version of Rome with the affluence afforded it. To this day, they continue to excavate more of this city. The task is enormous, expensive, and must be done with painstaking care and detail.

Before heading back to Rome, we stop at one of Sorrento's finest discotheques. I have never been to a discotheque before because I'm a minor and have no idea what to expect. By the time we arrive, the place is jumping and the dance floor is packed. Linda and I quickly join the dance floor and are thrilled when they play Lady Barbara. The other girls in our group aren't like us, and they don't speak or dance with anyone outside of the group. We don't care what the others think; we are having a great time and doing nothing wrong. I have one close friend, and that is all I need.

The excitement of the evening is cut short when we need to board the bus and head back to Rome, back to the monastery, and back to the monks. No more swimming, stunning sea vistas or sunbathing for a while. Back to those dreaded morning classes. It takes me over a week to remember how to say where I am living; well, most of it anyway. The name is Monastero di San Gregorio Magno al Celio, but all I can remember is San Gregorio. You would think I could at least learn the name of the place, but I'm having too much fun and know I am so far behind there isn't a chance I can catch up in a few weeks. Why ruin my vacation for something impossible to achieve?

A letter arrives from Mom. I can't believe how much she's writing that she misses me and how she misses my big mouth. She misses my big mouth AND she loves me! I can't believe she really misses me. Maybe I should try harder when I get home. I'll even try with my sisters. I wonder if it was difficult for her to write this. It doesn't appear that way, though. She's telling me that she hopes I meet nice girls and to watch out for the boys. "Please don't let me worry" and "please write," she pens. I remember, Mom; I remember!

23

At night when all of the dancing stops and we return to our rooms, I think about my friends and how much I miss them and wonder what they're doing. By the time I get to bed, they are just getting ready to go out with the time difference. Who have they met? Is he cute? Are they dating? I am missing it all, but then I remember what I'M doing.

The bus picks us up the next afternoon after class, and no one says where we're going. There are thousands of things to see in the Eternal City. We visit the Coliseum, and this time we get an actual tour of the inside. Our guide explains the sanguinary games that existed here, just like I've seen in the movies, and how it was famous for the fighting gladiators and for the persecutions of Christians. When they opened the Coliseum in 80 A.D., the opening ceremonies lasted for 100 days, and it is estimated that 9,000 wild animals were killed during these festivities to celebrate its dedication. After the dead animals were removed, the arena was often filled with water to actually stage naval battles. What a show! This was the entertainment the "government" was providing their people. All that blood; all those losses! A horrifying thought.

From a place with such a bloody history, our bus takes us to St. Peter's Square and the Vatican. The square is quite imposing with a size of nearly 700 ft. wide by 1115 ft. long. In the center stands an obelisk 82 feet high and is said to contain a relic of the Holy Cross on top. The Colonnade is considered to be Bernini's finest work and forms a beautiful entry to St. Peter's and the Vatican. Michelangelo, who served as main architect, designed the dome, and Bernini designed the great St. Peter's Square. On top of the colonnade are 140 statues of saints crafted by a number of sculptors between 1662 and 1703. As imposing as it all is, the two large wings opening like half circles seem like two outstretched arms of the temple receiving all mankind in one universal embrace. HE is welcoming you in.

Both raised Roman Catholic, Linda and I are excited about entering the Vatican. Walking up the majestic stairs nearly takes my breath away with anticipation. You enter through the portico where you are given a quick visual scan by the guards to see if your attire is appropriate to enter. Linda and I fail the test. Our arms aren't covered and our skirts too short. We are made to return to the bus and wait for the others.

It's worth the wait days later to see Michelangelo's La Pietà - The Virgin Mary is depicted cradling the dead body of Jesus on her knees. The Pietà is unique among Michelangelo's sculptures because it was the only one he ever signed. There is so much to see in the Vatican and the Sistine Chapel, but it's the Pietà that grabs my heart. You see Mary's sorrow, the deepest, most profound loss any person could experience, the loss of a child.

We return to the monastery to find the wall in front of the building lined with young Italian men. At first I thought this was a regular meeting place, but then I discovered that the guys wait there until us American girls come out and try to pick us up. It's actually cute; they are never pushy or inappropriate. They even befriended many of our American guys because they have never seen a Frisbee and end up playing with them for hours. It's great seeing them get along like this; something so trivial brought the two nationalities together – a simple game that doesn't even involve violence of any kind.

Another letter arrives from Mom. Boy, she must really miss me. It reads:

Dear Deb,

I hope you are doing fine. We are all ok at home.

Deb, I waited so patiently for a telegram and didn't get a letter until Friday. I was very happy to hear from you that you enjoyed the trip.

Deb, Richie has been calling me almost every day. He has been keeping me company some nights; he is the greatest. Deb, don't forget to send Aunt Anna a card. Roe got a letter today but Richie didn't. I called Aunt Mary up, and she gave me this address of my grandmother's people. It would be great if you could look them up.

Oh, Deb, it's so quiet around here; I miss you very much. Daddy is happy you are enjoying yourself, but Ma will just sit in the yard all summer.

Deb, the five dollars is for grandma's people from Aunt Mary. Their address is on the envelope. It would be great if you locate them.

Miss you,

Mother

Mom sends me five dollars for her grandmother's relatives SOMEWHERE near Naples. Five friggin dollars. Are you kidding me? I am going to have to spend the extra money I don't have in an attempt to find my great grandmother's relatives so that I could give them this five-dollar bill. Mom

26

thinks I can do anything; she thinks I can move mountains. Why wouldn't I be able to deliver five dollars to my great grandmother's birthplace on short notice? How would I get there, and how would we communicate? Oh, yes, Mom thinks I'm fluent in Italian. Why didn't she just arrange for another helicopter? But I know it's from her heart; this much I know.

Two weeks have gone by quickly, and we are just about ready to start moving onto our next stop for a while – so we think. I have spent the first two weeks buying everyone souvenirs. Mom is getting a statue of David; Grandma, a jade statue of the Blessed Mother holding Baby Jesus; Aunt Dee, a miniature white marble bird bath; Aunt Marie, a marble Blessed Mother; Dad gets a leather belt; Baby Joe, a toy; Baby Sal, who is yet to be born, gets a Sicilian cart and horse, and my two sister get miscellaneous items I liked along the way, and everyone gets medals, even the people who gave me a few dollars for spending money, they get metals, too. With all the souvenirs I'm buying, my spending money is dwindling quickly, and I still have four more weeks to go. I need to really put myself on a budget. I write Mom and tell her I'm almost out of money. She wants to know what's going on. It's not like I'm going to be homeless if I run out – *so I think*.

The mail comes and I actually get a letter from my sister, Mom's favorite. I can't believe how different my family is when there's an ocean between us. She writes all about the wedding and who of the cousins got drunk, but the next half of the letter says how she hated to see me go, how she's been crying ever since I left, and how she hates me being so far away. She pens, "even though I hate you, I love you," and "maybe when you get home we can act like sisters." She continues with: "do something bad so they send you home because this is the worse summer vacation I'll ever have." What have they done with my real sister?

27

After a day of touring, we are told to go to the dining room for a conference. Oh, they are probably going to tell us about our next move and what time to be ready. Everyone is assembled, and one of the guardians makes the shocking announcement: "As of this morning, your trip has been cancelled. The monastery will allow us to remain here for another two days and provide meals as well, but after that, you are on your own! Repeat, after two days, you are on your own!"

"Why?" we all clamor.

"We don't know," is their only response.

"That's it? You don't know!" we quickly respond.

Just like that, as if they're announcing the dinner menu. My mind races. My very first thought is we may be at war! Will I be able to get home? When? How will I live if I cannot get back to America? There's limited funds left and no phone service. I could never get Mom upset with this news. I don't have any information other than we are not proceeding with the trip. What would I tell her? How will I survive not knowing the language? Now I'm officially frightened. My mother definitely cannot handle this.

I look at Linda, and she's hysterically crying. Linda's had a very difficult life, which you'd never know from her personality, and I admire her a great deal because I think she can achieve anything on her own with her good looks, engaging personality, and endless energy. She lost her mom at a very young age and was raised by a wicked grandmother. Her dad walked out on his three kids when her mom was stricken with cancer and never returned. No one ever did anything for her, and fortunately she had some good friends and their families that loved her. This trip was extravagant for her. She wanted it as much as I did.

28

Might as well go to the Coliseum. This is what we've been doing since we arrived, and we don't know how much longer we'll be able to do it. My mind continues to spin out of control. I think, Oh, God, will we be forced to become one of those prostitutes who hang out there? How old will I be when I get back home? How will I possibly survive until then?

The information given to us 24 hours later is that the touring company, World Academy, filed bankruptcy, leaving approx. 6,000 students stranded throughout Europe. The questions still remain: how do we get home, and how do we provide for ourselves in the meantime? Still no answers. Mr. Zappola feels as badly as we do and takes us all out to dinner in Campo di Fiori, one of Rome's historic piazzas. We eat outside because it's magnificent, and the violin players keep stopping at our table to perform the classic Italian songs under the moonlight, and some of the students burst out crying when they begin to sing *Arrivederci Roma*. No one wants to say good-bye to Rome. We celebrate our new friendships tonight, the adventures we've had along the way, and most of all, we celebrate Rome. Rome has captured all our hearts, and we don't know when we'll be back, if at all. We don't even know **if** we will be leaving Rome at anytime in the near future.

I think about all the money Dad spent on this trip, and now I am coming home over three weeks early. Would he be upset with me for pushing him into paying for this trip, and now so much of it has been wasted? I'm unsure how Mom will feel, too. Is she going to be upset that I cut her quiet afternoons by the pool short? I've seen a different side of her these last few weeks through the mail. When I'm home, we all compete for her attention, and I resent getting the least of it, as I see it. If she really wants to know something she can't ask me, she'll ask Debbie, Jeanne, or Roberta.

My mother is loved by all my friends, who also call her mom. She has a relationship with each and every one of them, guys and girls, and they love it. She'll ask funny, personal questions about someone in the group, and they'll be hysterical. They're so amused by her colorful language because they don't hear it at home, and they don't have a relationship anything like this with their own mothers. I met Jeanne and Roberta while I was still in grammar school, and Debbie and I met sophomore year in Biology. Debbie is the only one I share many classes with and the only one who is also full blooded Italian. Being with her family doesn't seem too different than being with mine with all the company, food, and laughter. Mom has another benefit with my girlfriends: she can ask them things she can't ask me. We all do well in school, I'm in the top five percent of the class, but our driving force is our social life. I see my friends day and night, 365 days a year. The guys we regularly hang out with are several years older than us and attend a technical school. We have a bond between us that is unbreakable. We all love each other and love being together. We never fight. I am very happy that Mom really likes all my friends, but Mom is old-fashioned and doesn't even see any reason for me to go to college because she believes girls should just get married and have babies shortly after they graduate from high school. I have only one more year left, and she won't consider allowing me to go away to college - not a chance. And I won't consider going to a local college because I'd still be living at home, and the fighting would continue. I can't do this for another four years. Her biggest fear in life is having one of her daughters get pregnant before marriage. She told Aunt Margie she'd kill them and then kill herself. A murder/suicide. Not too dramatic!

She won't allow me to go off to college and yet somehow I get stuck in Rome! I head to bed after a late night dancing in the dining room, and a few hours later, there's a knock on my bedroom door. It's one of our "guardians." His message is strange and memorable: "There's a plane waiting for you in a few hours and .... have a nice life." Have a nice

LIFE. He just didn't know what to say to me, and he was happy to get rid of this possibly bad situation with me being a minor. The conversation feels so awkward and so wrong.

It's the middle of the night, and I have to leave at sunrise. I won't get a chance to say good-bye to anyone in the group except my roommate. I manage in a few short hours to pack my 40-day, 40-night wardrobe and get my belongings and myself to the front door long before anyone comes down for breakfast. I don't even get to say good-bye to Linda. She'll find out when she awakens; I assume the rest of the class will be flying home very shortly, too.

The last drive around the Coliseum tugs at my heart. Like an old love, I didn't get to say good-bye to this one. Would we meet again? I threw the coins into the Trevi, so, yes, I'm assured of coming back.

I arrive at the airport on barely any sleep and line up as I'm told. All I can think about is getting back to the United States now. How quickly that shifted! I can only imagine Mom's surprise; my friends' surprise! What a feeling of being detached from my country; what an indescribably bad, bad feeling. I'm going home to my mother's arms. Even though I haven't felt them around me very often, I know they'll be open when I arrive; this I know.

***

When we left Rome's Leonardo da Vinci Airport for New York City, I was seated next to a group of art students from the same travel company being escorted home. I was no longer in panic mode because my mom didn't know anything about this fiasco. My plan was to just show up, and I might even ring the doorbell for a real shocker. My mother's personality was over the top, so this would be perfect. I just needed to get home. I just needed to get to my front door before Mom found out. Other than the fact I was coming home early and Mom's quiet summer was cut short, they have not been affected by this bankruptcy.....so I thought.

The student next to me was also from New Jersey and lived not far from my home. As if my guardian angel set this up, she asked me how I was getting home. When I told her I didn't know, she offered a ride. I jumped at the offer. I felt safe considering she was from the same group and was going through the same experience of having her trip cut short. All the same, she was a complete stranger.

Landing at JFK to the sound of thunderous applause, some of us even kissed the ground when we walked off the plane. We were home; we were safe; and the phones worked. What a feeling! I knew then what it was to be an American!

I found my new friend from the plane and her dad who escorted me to a very comfortable Lincoln. My mind was racing, I was with complete strangers, and I was very anxious to see any landmark familiar to me when suddenly one appeared, the Montclair Golf Course. I knew I was only 10 minutes from home, and my heart started to race. Her dad was extremely kind and pleasant and asked me about my trip and home. At some point, he realized who I was and burst out: "You're the kid who they've been writing about in the newspaper." I knew what he meant. I had taken a photo op about the trip for a large newspaper before I left; I was the only kid from our county going. That's the story he's talking about. But then this complete stranger says to me: "Your mother is so worried." My mother is so worried! My mother is worried? And then I realized - MY MOTHER KNEW!!!

I braced myself as he told me about the last article when they interviewed my mother after the failure of the tour company. All that went through my mind was: I am so screwed. This was not like you forgot to call home and say you're going to be late for dinner. In an attempt to protect her, I actually did the opposite. Other than an occasional letter, she hadn't heard from me. I couldn't imagine what she went through, and I was more than afraid to find out!

We pulled up in front of my home, and her dad asked: "Can I come in with you? I'm dying to see your mother's face." "Sure." Part of me was thinking she might not go off on me if he's with me. It was the second week in July, dark out already, but not very late. My 15-year old sister was standing in front of the house with her new boyfriend. When she saw a strange car stop and then saw it was me, she ran and said she knew it was me; she said it had to be me. She was genuinely happy to see me, and I, her. The jealousy we lived with didn't appear at all that night. It was just love.

I walked up the cement walk to the front door. He took the heaviest of luggage and said he'd return to get the others. We were both anxious to see MOM! I have been afraid of her my whole life and rightfully so. But a good fear; a healthy fear. Dad worked too many long hours to be bothered with what his three daughters had going on. That was Mom's job. Even with her gregarious nature and Roseanne Barr type humor, she ran a tight ship when it came to how her daughters behaved. There was never a question in my mind if she would approve of something; I always knew. I never lied; never had to. I didn't know how long she had known about the "fall of Rome;" I NEVER CALLED HOME TO TELL HER!

At least I was dressed for her approval with my new big white brimmed hat and matching shoes I purchased next to the Trevi Fountain and was wearing the "negligee set" Aunt Francie gave me. Even though it was a negligee set, I passed it off as a beautiful lace outfit. It looked classy, Mom and I thought.

There was the issue of not learning Italian. I still didn't know the full name of the monastery, and I was home already. I remembered that I did, in fact, learn some; I learned how to sing the Coca-Cola commercial: *Tutto va bene con Cola-Cola, tutto va bene con Coke.* I was good.

I reached the top of the steps, and the door was unlocked as usual. My sister wasn't in for the night, and it was still early enough to be sitting with someone at the kitchen table enjoying coffee and cake. I opened the door, and to the far end of the house I saw Aunt Dee with her very pregnant belly at the kitchen table. She's like an older sister to me with her being only seven years older than I am. We went through a lot together especially since Uncle Sal, her husband, was injured in the service right before they were married. They gave him only a five percent chance of ever walking again, but gladly he fought the odds and started walking shortly after the operation. But those months at the veterans' hospital were difficult, and Dee and I would ride over every Wednesday night into the Bronx to visit him. I got to know his immediate family from Sicily very well, and his youngest brother was even my first real boyfriend. Shortly after they married, Aunt Dee became pregnant and moved into our second floor apartment. Their second baby was due to arrive in a matter of weeks.

Aunt Dee was facing me, and in front of her with his back to me was Uncle Sal. They were the only two people I saw. I yelled hello and got nothing. Absolutely nothing. I started to shake with worry. I yelled out another hello, and THEN my aunt recognized me. The big brimmed hat really threw her off, besides the fact I was supposed to be on another continent. She screamed out my name and wiggled herself out of the chair as quickly as she possibly could, belly first. While she was trying to get up, I heard a loud clang. Next thing I saw was my mother sprinting from behind the wall. She was standing next to the stove and was going to pour the steaming hot coffee she just made. Mom realized why Dee screamed my name and came screeching around the corner while I only made it as far as half way across the living room floor. The clanging I heard was my mom literally throwing the coffee pot from the hot stove into the sink when she heard my voice. She just needed to run.

She screamed something unrecognizable and grabbed me into a tight embrace. I never felt an embrace like that before. I never held her tightly either, and I enjoyed squeezing her back. What safer place than your mother's arms? Nowhere!

Mom broke her embrace, and it became loud quickly. I kissed Aunt Dee and Uncle Sal, and Mom kissed the man who drove me home. He quickly explained who he was and said he had to meet her and see the expression on her face. Mom explained that in all the excitement she thought I brought him home from Italy!!! What - a souvenir for her? She actually thought that even though I was too inconvenienced to call home in the last 17 days, I had no trouble bringing a man home.

It was a Friday night, and Dad would definitely be in bed already. His alarm goes off at 4:30 on Friday mornings, he drives to the Fulton Fish Market in New York City for fresh fish, and then drives back to his store in New Jersey. They are long and tiring days. I ran down the hall to their bedroom, knocked on the door and walked in. He was in a deep sleep, but I wanted to let him know I was home. I knew he had to be worried. I shook him gently, and he awakened quickly.

"Hi, Dad. It's me. I just wanted to tell you that I'm home," I gently whisper.

"You're home? How was your trip? Did you have a good time?" He mumbles back.

"It was great, Dad; great. Wait till I tell you about where I stayed; you're not going to believe it! I'll tell you tomorrow. Go back to bed; I just wanted to let you know I'm home," I assure him.

As he closed his eyes again, with a smile on his face, he says: "Okay. I'm happy you're home. Mommy was so worried."

I was a little taken aback when he says Mommy was worried, as if he didn't give it too much thought. As casual as missing one number on a bet that paid well that night. But I knew what he meant: he had LOTS of confidence in me. He always did.

"Good night, Dad; I'm home. Don't worry anymore. I'll give you your gift tomorrow."

My driver left, and the explaining commenced. Why hadn't I called? Mom said that the *Record Newspaper* telephoned her when they heard of the bankruptcy and remembered doing a story on me before I left. This was the first she heard of the situation and immediately went into panic mode. Who wouldn't be if your 17-year old kid was abandoned in a foreign country? And that was just the beginning of their worries; it got worse.

With 6,000 students stranded throughout Europe, I was lucky that I even had a chance to go on the trip. There were airplanes full of students ready to leave New York when they were told that their flight and entire trip were canceled. At least I got a 17-day Roman vacation. When my mom was told by the newspaper that the "hotel" was "relieving" us and we would no longer be provided with food and accommodations, she told him that she had received a letter from me stating I was running out of money and that she didn't know how she would be able to send me money. That phone conversation advising her of the demise of the trip and their interest in doing another story about me was nothing short of shocking, and her response sounded like my family didn't have much money. She was panic stricken just hearing the news. Mom immediately called the high school, and they knew nothing either. She had my itinerary and had Uncle Sal call the hotel in Rome. They informed him that I wasn't listed anywhere. It was more than two weeks into the trip, and the hotel had no record of me. That's because I WAS LIVING IN A MONASTERY.

Days go by and Mom never slept. Uncle Sal's brother, Placido, stopped by, and my mom showed him the photo of the monastery that I mailed home. Placido didn't have the name of the monastery, so he starts describing the building to the Italian telephone operator in the hopes SHE'D KNOW THE BUILDING HE'S TALKING ABOUT. Of course, they never find me.

Mom brewed plenty of coffee in those several days after the bankruptcy. People continued to stop by to offer support.

Mom's happiness washed away all that worry the moment she heard my voice. I was home and I was safe. But she wasn't letting me out of her sight for a moment. Not yet.

I jumped on the phone in between our mother-daughter conversation to call Richie. Mom said he had been worried and was constantly trying to comfort her. She started to tell me about all my friends and how they stopped by and sometimes went for a swim. That made her happy. So much was going on, and I was able to get the last 17 days of my friends' lives from my mother.

Richie's mom answered and was stunned to hear my voice. I told her to tell Richie I was home, and just minutes later I looked out my front door and heard the screeching of his tires coming from around the corner at the bottom of the hill. We stayed up for hours with my mom, repeating over and over the stories of Italy and how I ended up coming home so early. I just left out the part about Jerry and all the other guys except for Cesare who was not a romantic interest but a big part of my vacation.

After Richie left, Mom told me that she has other news: My bed had been promised to someone over the summer. A little girl from a less fortunate family near the store was invited by my parents to live with my family and be able to swim all summer in our pool until I returned in August. She went home for a few days and was returning to my room. My mother wanted me gone to have some peace and quiet, and what does she do, take another child in! Unlike me, I'm sure that younger child gave her no problems. I couldn't be mad, but I did want my own bedroom back at some point. My parents always showed me their compassionate side, so I wasn't surprised at all nor was I upset. I always felt fortunate, especially when I heard about some of Dad's customers.

Mom threw my dad out of the bed that night and made me sleep with her. She wasn't letting me go. I hadn't slept with her since I was an infant, but I hopped into her bed without any argument. I couldn't imagine sleeping with Mom knowing how she practically slept on top of my dad. She was such a tough sleeper, and I was used to sleeping alone. She would always have her left leg, which wasn't delicate, draped over my father's body while they slept. It was closer than spooning; it was suffocating, I thought. I couldn't imagine being able to sleep with her leg covering me like that. But that's the way they always slept. But that night I had to sleep with her, and I wasn't fighting the idea. She wouldn't drape her leg over me like she did Dad. Mom loved to talk, and I could certainly talk about Italy or my friends. I wanted to talk about it all, and I was so pumped on adrenaline. But Mom wasn't into talking. She was exhausted and just wanted to sleep. As she lay right next to me, spooning me, she draped her arm over my body and fell asleep. Once she was settled in and comfortable, she rolled her left leg over my body for the duration of the sleep. That dreaded leg. I didn't fight that either that night. The tight embraces, the same bed, the conversations, all of it was special that night. I was home. I was safe in my mother's arms, even if I hadn't remembered what they felt like.

That night after dinner I walked back up to Franklin School where the group would always meet. It was a joyous reunion. I got to tell everyone over and over again of my incredible trip and my sudden departure from the country. It was all so exciting. Everyone wanted to know the very same thing: How's your mother?

***

On my 18th birthday, Mom sat me down. She never sat me down before; she'd sooner knock me down, and told me it was time I seriously think about getting married. Two weeks later I broke it off with Richie.

Many years would pass, and my sister, her husband, and three children would come to live on the second floor when Aunt Dee and her family moved to the next town. One day her youngest girl, Desi, six years old, was sitting at our kitchen table, and we were all discussing learning other languages in school. I impressed Desi with my ability to count from 1 to10 in French. Then I mentioned that I could sing the Coca-Cola song in Italian. With that, my mother yells out: "She's teasing you, Desi; she doesn't know how to sing in Italian." I replied: "Oh, yes, I can." So, she says: "Sing it." With that, I sang, *"Tutto va bene con Coca-Cola; tutto va bene con Coke."* Mom couldn't believe her ears and asked me how I knew it, and I tell her all these years later that it was from my trip in high school. Without moving a muscle in her body other than her arm, she grabs the phone to call Aunt Dee and tell her that I could actually sing in Italian. Of course, Aunt Dee didn't believe it either, and Mom handed me the phone and says to sing. I belt out my long rendition of the Coca-Cola commercial. Dee was as shocked as Mom and says, "Very good." I cannot believe they are making such a big deal of this. IT'S ALL OF FOUR WORDS, four friggin words! My mother says to Dee: "I told you she is fluent in Italian." She could ALWAYS make me laugh.

About the five dollar bill Mom sent me to get to my great grandmother's family, it would be many years before I would find and meet them in Sant' Arsenio and Polla, Italy.

Chapter Two

What Not to Wear When Crossing the Alps - A Lesson in Stupidity

Life at Home: 1974

I'm working as an executive secretary during the day and waitressing in the evenings to earn extra money to return to Italy. I want to get back so badly I even considered selling my Corvette until Uncle Joe brought me to my senses. Not surprising, Mom and I are still not getting along. I'm 21, and she's still pushing me to get married. My sister Nicey is 19 and married her childhood sweetheart last year, a mere week after graduating high school. They're expecting their first child. I've been going steady with Kevin, who lives only two blocks away, for a year now. We hung with the same crowd for several years until he started to date someone out of the area, and I rarely saw him. After four years, a chance meeting with me evolved into a romance. He's 23, lives at home, and works with his mother in his uncle's business. So, he sees his mother day and night. She's very disappointed in Kevin because he left this girlfriend of four years, the girl she loves like a daughter, to be with me. His mother is so upset that I'm never invited or welcomed in their home. Yet, STILL, my mom is pushing for a wedding, while I'm happy the way things are and want to travel with my friends. I couldn't consider traveling with any guy because I wouldn't be allowed back in my home if I did.

It's been four years since my last trip to Italy, and I'm obsessed with finishing the tour that ended so abruptly. With Kevin in my life, I don't get to hang out with my friends like before, no more clubbing. Jeanne got married two years ago, but merely 13 months after the wedding, her husband was tragically killed in a multi-car pileup on the New Jersey Turnpike, leaving her widowed at the age of 22. Debbie is single and has no ties, so it will be the three of us going together this time. We won't travel with a touring company after my last fiasco; I'll be the guide. The only reservations we have are for our flights, a car rental, and a room for the very first night in Rome through a travel agency. Our plan is to drive ourselves to our destinations and find hotels along the way. Except for Paris, we plan to visit the cities originally on my agenda in 1970, plus we added Sicily to visit Uncle Sal's relatives, a must-see! We have nearly <u>four weeks</u> to drive from Rome to Sicily and then turn around and drive back up the entire country to cross the Alps into Switzerland.

Kevin is not thrilled about my vacation plans, but he has no choice. He'll stay busy with Jeanne's new boyfriend, Eddie, while we're gone. She started seeing Eddie not too long after her husband was killed, and they're already in love. All of our parents are happy we are doing this trip together because the three of us are all levelheaded, so there doesn't appear to be much concern from any of them. Yet, all of our siblings are more than happy to get rid of us. None of our parents have been to Italy or Sicily, so they, too, don't know what we should expect. Before leaving home, we decide that one of us would call home each week, and the families would call each other. I wasn't going to make the same mistake twice.

***

In Rome we spend just a few days sightseeing the Coliseum, Roman Forum, Trevi Fountain, Pantheon, and, of course, The Vatican. I'm anxious to show my friends San Gregorio, the monastery, and the courtyard where I attended class in 1970. Climbing the hill, I bring them right to the beautiful courtyard. It's more beautiful than I remembered. At the other end of the portico, there's a man standing alone. I pay him no attention, but suddenly Debbie screams for us to leave quickly because the man is not just standing there, he's masturbating while looking at us. All of this right outside the church door where I used to take my classes!

We have an ambitious schedule driving from Rome all the way to the southern tip of Italy, ferry over to Sicily, drive deep into the mountains to visit Uncle Sal's family, ferry back to Italy the same day before heading north. I'm the only one who really knows how to drive a stick shift; Jeanne and Debbie practiced a few times at home. Regardless, we are going to share the time behind the wheel and have relatively little fear about any of it.

Before reaching Sicily, we'll visit Naples, Sorrento, Capri, and Pompeii. We don't have directions; we're just follow the signs. I'm driving, Debbie is riding shotgun, and Jeanne is in the back. None of us speak or read Italian, and we really are having difficulty understanding the signs. If we could read better, we'd realize that the exit we take in Naples is actually for the port. Lost in the toughest part of this big city, we stop a young man for directions. Jeanne and Debbie roll down their windows for all of us to hear. He seems pleasant enough, and while he's speaking, we are all concentrating on trying to understand anything he's saying. Suddenly, his voice changes, his pitch climbs, and his arm bursts through the window as he attempts to grab a handbag on the backseat. Fortunately, Jeanne is able to grab the strap of the bag and jerk it back inside, and the young man quickly flees. Besides money, the bag has our passports. We hadn't anticipated or prepared for something like this, and now there's fear looming.

Family members warned us of the price of gasoline in Italy. It is ridiculously expensive, triple what we pay in the States. How could anyone afford to operate a car at these prices? We have about five hours or more of driving nearly every day, and even with the three of us sharing the expense, something would have to go. It's not going to be souvenirs; I'm not going home empty handed. We'll have to settle on more moderately priced hotels and curtail where and what we eat. If all I can afford is Gelato and Coke, I'll be happy. I'm in friggin Italy! And there's ALWAYS pizza.

We arrive in beautiful and vibrant Sorrento where the people are very friendly and less rushed than the Romans. Lemon groves and leisurely cafes pepper the landscape. Live music can be heard throughout the streets, as people are dining outdoors under the lights of the moon and the city. We perform our same routine of having one of us run into the lobby to check out the rates and availability. Fortunately, we quickly find suitable lodging, *Hotel Mediterraneo*, overlooking the Bay of Naples. It's July and the nights feel like it's still daylight from the warmth of the still, night air. The hotel has a great pool located at a distance, so the three of us decide to go for a relaxing night swim. The whole idea sounds magnificent after such a stressful ride from Naples. The water feels incredibly refreshing after all this heat, and then suddenly we see something strange. There are low flying birds circling above us. Initially, we think it's beautiful, but it very quickly becomes frightening when we notice the span of their wings and realize they're bats! The three dingbats - and I do mean us - mortified, run screaming from the pool into the lobby dripping wet and fly into an elevator. How is it there's no sign "Beware of Bats"? Were we supposed to know this?

We tour Pompeii and quickly walk through the ruins under the blazing sun. There is no escaping the tortuous heat; no covers, no trees, no shade. We cannot consider a private guide, but we're able to mingle in with a tour group. Pompeii was considered a resort town, and many of its villas and apartments were designed for wealthy visitors. The carvings on the walls tell much: A painting of a fish indicates it's a fish market, fruits and vegetables for a grocery store, etc. They had plenty of public spots for parties, including a generously-sized brothel where anthropologists have found a lot of obscene graffiti such as public mosaics depicting extremely graphic sex and penis decorations on street corners. A picture of a penis indicated how to find the brothels at the edge of the city. Inside the brothel, the rooms were full of paintings of different sexual positions so a customer could just point to the chosen preference and select someone to enjoy it with. But because we're females, we're not allowed in to see the most graphic. There were also public baths, an arena, gladiators' barracks, restaurants, and even a hotel. The most famous aspect of Pompeii's ruins is no doubt the hundreds of plaster casts that archeologists have made of the volcano's victims. When the ash poured down over the city in 79 AD, people were killed instantly. Their remains were preserved in plaster, eerily in the exact poses they struck when they noticed their impending doom, terrified facial expressions and all. As their bodies decomposed, they left perfectly-formed hollows in the ash.

At dinner, some guys around our age come over to our table and begin a conversation with the little English they know and invite us to join them after eating. Had they been Americans and we met in the States, we probably would accept an invitation to meet them again, but this is not the United States, and we are definitely not going to leave each other. One of the guys tries talking Debbie into going to see Mount Vesuvius with him after dinner. How unique; how many other ladies can say they've gotten such an invitation? Actually, in this town, millions! Debbie declines, but we laugh all the way back to the hotel as Debbie goes on a rant explaining that Mount Vesuvius was not what he was really looking for her to see erupt!

The following morning we take a hydrofoil boat to Capri and jump into a rowboat that will take us to the famous Blue Grotto, a sea cave on the coast and Capri's largest attraction. The sunlight, passing through an underwater cavity and shining through the seawater, creates a blue reflection that illuminates the cavern. We wait nearly an hour to enter the cavern with the small boats rocking back and forth over the large swells crashing against them. The captains of these small vessels entertain you by singing popular Italian songs just like on the gondolas in Venice. As we enter the small opening, there's a large rope, like a clothes line, hanging from above. The captains grab hold of it so their boats don't crash against the sides, meanwhile we lay nearly completely flat not to hit our heads as we enter. The water inside is stunning with a color blue I have never seen. All of the Mediterranean is stunning with its seemingly dozens of shades of blues and greens, all God's work. This must be His pool, and we're allowed to visit this day.

We arrive back on land and take a bus to the very top of the island, Anacapri. If we make a right at the top of the steps, we can find the single chair, cable car ride that will take us descending through people's yards before ascending to the summit. Debbie and Jeanne are afraid of heights, but to my surprise, they both want to go. We are so close to the homes, we hear their conversations, and I secretly wish they'd invite us in to see how they live, see how they cook, "feel" like an Italian instead of an Italian American, but I know it's merely a fantasy; we don't even speak their language.

Uncle Sal says his place of birth is only about an hour or so from the port once we arrive onto the island. It's such an incredibly long way to go just to say hello to my aunt's in-laws, but because my friends are very fond of Uncle Sal, they agree to go. Of course, I hear the moaning and groaning all the way - and I do mean ALL the way!

Uncle Sal was the oldest of four children. When he was a young boy, his father moved to the United States and lived with his sister, leaving the rest of the family behind while he saved money to send for them a few years later. Uncle Sal was given to a farmer to work as a farmhand nowhere near his home and ended his education in Sicily. He slept in the barn with the animals and only saw his family at Christmastime until he left Sicily at the age of 16. When the day came for the family to leave, all four kids went to every home in the village to say good-bye. When they arrived in America, he resumed his education. By the time he reached eighth grade, he was driving to school. He eventually went on to receive his civil engineering degree, but only after serving in the U.S. Army, got married and had his first son.

As we continue south to Reggio Calabria, we can see from the highway how the towns are changing. They are not garish, and there are many farms that appear to be small, the size a family could sustain on their own. From our view, there doesn't appear to be any wealth here compared to the towns to the north. But we can also see the stunning and vibrant colors of the sea. We find a very modest hotel near the port and rise early to catch a ferry with our car. Since this is a day trip, we leave our luggage at the hotel. I've heard about Sperlinga since I was a little kid. Aunt Dee met Uncle Sal when she was just a teenager, and they would come to our home for dinner once a week. We loved hearing his stories of the old country. The most amazing part was the fact that their home was actually a cave that they shared with their chickens. It's the 20th century, and everyone finds it hard to believe people in this century still live in caves. My father never believed it, so now we're going to see if it's what he says. The story of living in a cave is what impels us to drive the distance.

I met Uncle Sal's Uncle John when visiting the United States, and I'm fairly certain he'll remember me. He doesn't speak a word of English, but I'm confident someone will. I asked Uncle Sal for Uncle John's address, and he would always say the same exact thing: "It's the fourth house on the left." How could I possibly know where the first house begins in a town?

We leave the hotel in Reggio Calabria to drive to the ferry, and when we reach our *macchina*, car, there's a note on our windshield that reads: "We will be waiting for you." Who are they, and why are they waiting for us? Both Jeanne and Debbie are frightened, and now they are getting me wound up. We cannot figure out how EVERYONE knows we're Americans. We're deliberately wearing blue jeans like the rest of the world, and I hide my bleached blonde hair under a denim cap. Jeanne and Debbie do the same. No matter where we go, we are pointed out as Americans. I keep looking at our rental to see if it indicates *Americani*, but I see nothing.

After a short ferry ride, we reach Sicily, and I feel a great deal of emotions, having both my father's parents born here. I don't know where in Sicily, I have a sense of coming home regardless. We retrieve our car from the ferry and begin our journey to Sperlinga from the directions we receive at the port. We expect to be there by lunchtime, stay a few hours, and return to the ferry, arriving back in Reggio Calabria before dark because "they will be waiting for us." Debbie and Jeanne are too frightened to return in the dark.

Sicily has magnificent beaches all around the island, but once we get away from the coast, it's all mountainous terrain. We drive for hours with a vast amount of empty space in between each village. I recall Uncle Sal saying his mom was from Nicosia, the town next to Sperlinga, merely six miles away, and yet they spoke an entirely different dialect. His parents even had a hard time understanding each other. We have never seen anything like this before. Growing up in Northern New Jersey, each town just blends into the next. It is almost impossible to distinguish where one town ends and the other begins. I feel like I'm lost in a Western movie given the absence of buildings or people and surrounded by mountains as we ride from village to village on unpaved roads.   I'm in a spaghetti western!   We continue on our path. We had come all the way from Rome, and it didn't make sense to turn back now. How much further could it be if Uncle Sal says an hour and a half from the port? Answer: four hours!

Finalmente, we reach the end of the long dirt road and enter Sperlinga. There on the second floor balcony is Uncle John. It's the fourth house on the left. There is no mistaking it.

Uncle John recognizes me, but no one here speaks English. School will be getting out soon, and we will have to wait for Cousin Pina. We quickly realize, however, she speaks much less English than we had hoped. We keep trying to explain that we want to see Uncle Sal's cave, but she thinks we are asking to see the medieval fortress which is in ruins. We go through a quick tour of this once impregnable fortress by crossing what used to be a drawbridge, not understanding one thing she is pointing out to us, and then we climb the 80 stone staircase to the top and get a stunning 360 degree view. We can see for miles. I'm loving every minute of this, but Debbie and Jeanne are getting very restless. We have to make the long trip back to the port, and we still haven't seen Uncle Sal's cave. I tell them I'm sure we can spend the night and leave early the next day, but they insist on getting back because our luggage is there.

After many hand gestures and attempts at using the few Italian words I know, Pina finally understands, and we walk the few blocks to the cave. It's nothing like I expected. It's a rock covering a good portion of the town where people have carved out a section to create a home, each with its own entrance and address. And they are multistory units. Some are three levels, and when you climb the stairs to the top bedroom, you're on a different street. Story has it that my uncle's father chiseled the rock to create his second floor. The first floor housed the kitchen, which they shared with their chickens, and the second floor consisted of one large room with a stone wall on one side in the back that separated two beds. His parents slept on one side, and all four children slept in the other bed on the other side of the stone wall. Standing in this room, I feel like I'm in Bedrock and the Flintstones live next door. Off of this bedroom is a balcony that gives you an incredible view of the valley below.

There was no electricity when Uncle Sal was growing up, nor did they have indoor plumbing. Mima, Sal's only sister, a little girl at the time, had the job of hauling water from the well to the home. But today, they have all these utilities. The walls are covered in wood paneling, and the floors and steps are covered in marble. The cabinets are made of fine wood, and the armoire in the bedroom is so large and ornate that it's constructed in the room itself. In the kitchen, there's a long string draped across the room that hangs the homemade pasta. Typical of Italians, flowers adorn the balconies and the entrances to the homes and also hide many imperfections, while the Italian soil and climate bless them in great abundance. It's not necessary to have fancy planters; Italians will use anything from old pails to broken down washing machines. If they have a hole and can hold dirt, it can be used as a planter.

Debbie and Jeanne have grown impatient and show no restraint in hiding their feelings. As I'm lagging behind with Pina, they are running ahead in an effort to get me moving faster. By now, the word has spread throughout the town that *Americani* are here, and people start pouring out, especially the young boys. Heading back to Uncle John's, a bunch of young boys start following us, yelling, "*puttana*." Is it the halter tops we're wearing or the high platform shoes that give them that impression? Or is it merely because we are Americans? Walking down the long, wide, stone steps near Uncle John's, we see cousin Nino, the town shepherd, coming to greet us with his sheep, and they are following him down the long staircase like obedient dogs.

The clutch in the car is very weak after all the abuse it's getting from Debbie and Jeanne, and we never know what to do with the manual choke. Do we open or close it? When we climb a hill, the car is having more and more difficulty, and we're climbing at an extremely slow pace. It's so slow that now the young Italian boys are chasing us on foot while we're driving up the hill! It's THAT slow.

We've seen what we came for, and now we must start heading back to catch the last ferry. We say our good-byes to the relatives, and Cousin Nino gives us an entire wheel of Provolone cheese to carry back home for Uncle Sal. We thank them for their hospitality, stow the unpacked cheese in the trunk, and begin our long trip back to the port. Unfortunately, the cheese wheel will never make it to America. Around

Naples, the stench permeating from the trunk becomes so overwhelming that Debbie pulls over and tells us she's not going one more inch with the cheese and proceeds to dump the entire wheel under a tree! We can't stop her. Now, who is going to tell Uncle Sal?

We make it back to the hotel without incident. No one is waiting.

We anxiously drive north and have no plans as to where we'll stop. We ride the main highway, A1, all the way to Florence, a nearly 300-mile trip, and arbitrarily choose an exit to look for the night's accommodations. Taken by its beauty, we reserve a room at Villa La Massa, a grand 16th-century Medici estate on 22 acres of gardens set among the Tuscan Hills and perched on the banks of the Arno River. This place is so magnificent, we can't walk away. It's well above our budget, but all three of us make the decision to stay two nights regardless. Dining in their garden on this actual Renaissance estate, river flowing immediately below us, is breathtaking. We are awe struck by the lavishness of it all; it's like we're in a movie.

By now, our funds are really low, and we are counting every lire. When we first arrived in Italy, we ate in nicer restaurants, but no matter where we went, it was never as good as my mom's. Debbie is the toughest person in the world to please. She doesn't like anything with red sauce except pizza, nor does she eat fish. It's hard to believe her mom is such a great Italian cook. So we eat our meals at the Auto Grills, a high end cafeteria, on A1 all the way up to Venice.

Venice is beautiful - but expensive. We are able to get a room at Hotel Trovatore, a mere few blocks from the main piazza, Piazza San Marco. It's not Hotel Danieli where the movie stars stay, but it's more than adequate. We wander around Venice's labyrinth of passages and window shop. It's the only kind of shopping we can afford in this city. Another strike; this time it's garbage. I don't know which is worse. Even though the garbage strike detracts from the obligatory gondola ride we treat ourselves to, I could never consider coming to Venice and not experience this. In addition to garbage, dead rats are floating on the water. We stay a couple of nights and then exit the city via water taxi for our next destination, Milan, a city I know nothing about.

We're riding for several hours when we realize that we left our passports at the hotel in Venice, and we can't check into another hotel without them. We can't afford the extra gas and the expense of another water taxi, so we make the executive decision to go straight onto Milan and to the American Embassy for help. We fail to consider that it's Sunday, and the Embassy is closed. The police station is our only remaining option.

We arrive in Milan and drive to a police station and explain our situation. The officer advises us that he has a friend with a hotel and we could stay there until our passports arrive in the mail. We're extremely relieved until the hotel turns out to be a first class dump - no air conditioning - and they will only provide us with separate rooms on different floors. Left with no choice, we pay for the two rooms, but the three of us sleep in one bed out of fear. Late that night our phone rings, and it's the police officer calling to see if we would join him and his friend who owned the hotel. By now, we trust no one and decline his invitation. We also worry if he or his friend would try something. Who would we call if it's the police giving us trouble? We became suspicious from the beginning when they tried to separate us. We suffer at night in the sweltering heat, three of us in one bed, screams coming from the floor above us. We are scared. Our only weapon is a butter knife that Debbie sleeps with! We have no choice but to stay until the passports arrive. We're in a city famous for its high fashion and even higher prices.   Having no interest in going to one more church or cathedral, we take a day touring Lake Como, an upscale resort area known for its dramatic scenery, its deep blue water set against the forested foothills of the Alps. The stunning Mediterranean villas with their formal gardens, long, winding staircases leading to their private docks hugging the lake are stunning.   Hundreds of years old, the villas still scream opulence.   It looks more like an oil painting than anything real.

Five days pass for the passports to arrive, not one second too soon, and we are gone the very first moment they reach us. The sun is blazing hot, and we haven't had relief from the heat in nearly a week. The three of us are wearing short-shorts, halter tops, and platform shoes again because of the extreme heat, and we're ready to cross the Alps into Switzerland. It's not long before we notice that the weather is changing quickly, actually, precipitously, from extreme heat to a mere 20 degrees above freezing.   There's snowcapped mountains immediately in front of us, and here we are clothed for the beach! Jeanne is running into several hotels inquiring about rates and quickly returns because they're out of our price range. I'm mortified; we're a friggin freak show!

 Because we have no winter clothing, we don't venture outdoors much and do any sightseeing from the car in Interlaken, another beautiful lake resort town in central Switzerland with the landscape of the Alps as their backdrop, and admire the beautiful chalets.

Jeanne is driving over the famous Lucerne Bridge. I'm in the backseat, and Debbie is riding shotgun. Suddenly, Jeanne turns her head to look at something and rear ends a Mercedes. She hits the Mercedes so hard, our radiator is laying on the bridge. It's such a spectacle, passersby are taking photographs.   Fortunately, no one is hurt. Once again, we're talking to the police. We could go years never speaking with police, and yet we have managed to call on them twice this week. We're taken to their station where we're informed that if we don't pay the fine immediately, other accommodations will be provided for us behind bars. Against our will, we pay.

***

Soon after arriving home, Kevin gave me an ultimatum: get married or he would leave me. Mom and I were getting along for the first time because she saw hope of me getting married, and marriage was the only way a good Italian girl leaves her family. To keep the harmony, I reluctantly agreed to the marriage. I had wanted to move out on my own, but I was afraid I'd lose my entire family; I thought especially about my grandmother and knew I couldn't do it. I set the wedding date 18 months away, a lifetime away, but as the date got closer and closer, I wanted out. I tried to postpone it when Mom's sister, Aunt Marie, had open heart surgery scheduled five days before the wedding, but Kevin wouldn't hear of it. And the chemistry wasn't there like it was with my ex Jimmy. I wanted Mom to say that if I didn't love him enough I should cancel the wedding. I cried the night before, confessing I didn't want to go through with it, but she still said nothing - absolutely nothing. It was probably because of the big church wedding, the 18 attendants, and the nearly 300 people expected. It would have been more drama than even she could have handled. Her goal had always been to marry me off, and the sooner, the better. My "draw" was the horse drawn carriage I hired to transport me from home to the church, part of my childhood dream of living on the Ponderosa.

On the morning of the wedding, it rained hard, and everyone kept saying it was good luck. When Dad went into the basement that morning, he found it had flooded; it had NEVER flooded before. So, on what was supposed to be the happiest morning of my life, Dad and I spent hours scooping up water until we were dry. Only a few hours later, he walked me down the aisle to what should have been my happily ever after. Water was coming from above and from below. I was already drowning. At the end of the reception when they announced last call, Mom ran up to the bar and ordered four

Scotches - for herself! She had been waiting for this for years, and she was going to party all night long!

Ironically, once I got married, Mom and Dad insisted I still come to lunch every day as I had done all along. It would actually upset her if I didn't come. Had she forgotten she pushed me out? I never discussed any problems with my marriage with her or anyone else. We never had the intimacy I had with Jimmy, no tenderness. I thought my unhappiness was normal even when I would have to run out of the grocery store and go home to cry. I thought I was just too tired. Going home after the wedding, to my parents' home, I kissed them whenever I walked in and whenever I left, as if they were any other relatives and not my parents. It felt strange and sad because it made me feel as if it was no longer my home. Kissing them was nice because I was showing respect, certainly more than when I was single, and I knew we should have been doing this all long. Both were always very happy to see me, and with Dad being retired, he'd often barbeque me a filet mignon for lunch. I fell in love with steak that summer. Things had certainly changed with us. It appeared they were having regrets over pushing me out. I felt lost!

Jeanne married her new boyfriend Eddie shortly after we returned from Italy.

Debbie married Al a year after I said my I Do's.

Dad, along with his entire crew, was arrested for booking numbers and was reprimanded to a rehab center, a home, belonging to St. Lucy's Church in Jersey City. He left on Halloween Day to serve his sentence and was released on January 2nd of the following year, just 63 days. They did, however, allow him to come home for Christmas Eve given

Dad never had any other violation in his life. Fortunately, by the time his case came to court, he had already retired and sold his business. He never booked another number again. But during those 63 days, on Sundays, I'd take a cooked pot of meatballs and gravy and drive through the Holland Tunnel into Little Italy to buy cannoli and bring everything to the rehab home for him and the crew. Dad was always allowed to leave and purchase the Italian bread himself.

Chapter Three

Life at Home: 1993

I'm single again. No surprise. We stayed married for over three years, and all that time my relationship with my mother-in-law remained fragile. I loved my mother, but I blamed her for pushing me into this unhappy marriage. The rain on our wedding day wasn't good luck, and I should have realized that the flooding in our basement on that morning was a bad omen.

My parents believed in God and being a good Christian, but they themselves were not church goers. Regardless, I was sent to Catholic school for my first six years of education and attended mass six days a week. As a very young kid, I hated it. The mass was said in Latin with the priest's back to us, and we were made to kneel perfectly straight in the pews for long periods of time. I was frightened of the nuns, and they were never kind to me. After we moved and I was able to attend public school, I stopped attending mass. But when faced with a divorce, the first place I returned to was the church. Even with no love lost between my husband and me, I was lost and humiliated over a failed marriage. Returning to church was very emotional, bringing back so many bad memories from childhood, and combined with the stress of the divorce, I sobbed each time I knelt down to pray. Sometimes I couldn't control myself, and I'd have to leave. Debbie and Jeanne were there for me every day. Only with them could I laugh again. Mom was devastated, too, but I think for different reasons. She knew I blamed her for pushing me into

59

it, and she quickly saw how he changed once I became his wife. He didn't want my family around; he wanted to control me. Once she recognized that, Mom wanted me back home. I never did go; instead I purchased my first condominium a week after the divorce became final, not one cent came from my ex husband, and I continued the tradition of eating with my family every Sunday like any honorable Italian daughter. I was unhappy and embarrassed, and I was making Mom unhappy. It wasn't at all what I wanted.

A year later I began attending a local university while working full time, receiving my bachelor's degree in Business Administration seven years later in 1988 with full honors - only four months after Mom passed. Just prior to graduation, I began a new career in the mortgage business. Thankfully, Mom lived to see things begin to prosper for me, and I was very happy that I could start to help her a little financially. Mom willed herself to live long enough to see my sister receive her law degree, but not me. I resented her for that, especially since it was such a long and difficult struggle for me as well. My graduation day would be one of the saddest days of my life.

Dad is now living on his own. Mom's been gone for five years, and still I never miss a Sunday at his home. I cook, clean, do his laundry, and pay his bills every weekend. If I want to go into New York City to shop, he comes with me, and we share a memorable Sunday afternoon together. He is 78 years old and recently had a terrible scare when he passed out in the shower from a drop in his blood sugar, suffering second and third degree burns on his body. From his hospital bed, he asks me to take him to Sciacca to find the home his mother was born in Sicily. Dad had never expressed any interest in going anywhere except Florida, so when he asked me to take him to find his mother's birthplace, I thought it was merely because he felt a sense of mortality at that moment and it would pass. A few weeks later, he mentioned it again, and I knew he was serious. I'm doing relatively well, so the entire vacation is on me. I'm proud I can do this for him, and I'm elated to be sharing the experience of finding my grandmother's home with him. I will be turning 40 on the trip, so it's a perfect idea. This time we'd take a tour because it would be easier traveling with him. One week in Italy and one week in Sicily.

Before leaving, I ask Dad to take me to his mother's grave who passed when I was two years old. Grandma had 11 children, Dad being somewhere in the middle, and I'm told she would have liked to have 11 more. When Dad was drafted into the Army during WWII, he was stationed in Iceland. He didn't smoke or drink, and the only thing he spent money on was gambling - craps, to be specific. From his winnings, he was able to send $10,000 to his mother for herself. When the war was over and he returned home, to his surprise, she had purchased for him a building with a grocery store and six apartments instead of keeping the winnings for herself. Dad was devoted to her even after her death and went to the cemetery regularly. I hadn't been there since I was a very young child, and now I'm going to pay my respects after all these decades. I'm embarrassed as I stand at her grave over this, and I tell her that I'm taking her son to Sicily, to Sciacca, and wished she would see to it that we'd have a great trip.

In 1986, my sister called to tell me a letter arrived for me from Italy. The writer says we met at the San Gregorio monastery in 1970, and when he came across my old letters, feelings of warmth had rushed over him, and he was attempting to find me. He further wrote that he had become the top physician in all of Italy. It was Cesare 16 years later. When I knew I was returning with Dad three years later, I wrote and gave him my itinerary.

***

Dad and I arrive at the airport and find two chairs while waiting to board. A very nice gentleman near Dad's age, Jerry, is seated next to us and tells us that he owns the Italian bakery in the same town we live. He asks our names, and when I give him my last name, my ex-husband's last name, he keeps repeating, "I don't believe it; I don't believe it!" I can't imagine what stirred this excitement, and then he says, "Your ex-mother-in-law is my girlfriend"! My ex-mother-in-law! I can't believe my ears. Fourteen years have passed, but the memory of her and the ill feelings resurface at this moment like the expression on her face as I walked down the aisle on my wedding day. It was as if she was in mourning.

Jerry is sitting alone, and my first thought is that she is in the bathroom and she's going on the tour. I've waited 19 years to return to Italy, and now this! I start to shake until he tells me he's only been dating her a few weeks and is traveling with his two grandsons, Little Jerry, 30 years old, and Anthony, 20, who are in the bathroom. Had he started seeing her a few weeks earlier, she would be with us, he says. Thank you, Jesus!

We reach our hotel in Rome. While waiting in line at the reception, I notice a distinguished man in the lobby reading a newspaper. A minute later someone taps me on the shoulder, and when I turn, it's the same distinguished man. He says to me, "Debora?" I'm stunned; how could he possibly know my name? He says, "I'm Cesare." Cesare? I can't believe it. The last 19 years have been good to him. His short, very curly hair is now longer, and the curls are loose. My memory of him is short and stocky, but that is not him now. His look is very European, and it suits him well.

Cesare came to the hotel to invite me to lunch, a rare break from his very demanding schedule. I hadn't planned on meeting him looking like I hadn't slept in days, so I just run to the room and freshen up quickly. This will give Dad a chance to rest while I'm gone for a few hours. We're enjoying a great lunch, and with the wine giving Cesare liquid courage, he tells me that he had always wanted to "jump my bones" all those years ago. I'm shocked; I always thought he was interested in Linda; I thought everyone was interested in Linda. Over lunch, he tells me that before accepting the highest medical position in this country, he relocated his family to Africa for six years to open a small hospital. It was his way of giving back. He is arguably the leading authority in the world on socialized medicine and is sought after by many countries for his advice. We speak of the Pope, and he tells me that he oversees his medical needs and knows him personally. Cesare and his wife have a home in the country like many Italians, but his apartment in Rome is owned by the Vatican. He says with a big laugh, "The Pope is my landlord." I laugh thinking how a person would tell the Pope they'll be late with the rent. It's still funny to him, too. I'm with such an interesting and accomplished man, and I feel honored how he feels about me.

My hotel is located on a busy Roman street not far from San Gregorio where we met, and he wants to say a somewhat proper good-bye. He pulls his BMW onto the sidewalk and kisses me good-bye. I get out, and he quickly makes a U-turn on the sidewalk. Only the Italians! When I return to the hotel, Dad says, "Too bad you didn't meet him before his wife." I'm shocked and say, "Dad, I was 17!" I'm wondering if he still thinks I should have stayed and married Cesare. I wonder, too, how Mom would have felt. She wanted me out of the house, but she'd never want me that far away...... This I know.

When I awaken the following morning, Dad is not in the room. An early riser, he must have gone down to the lobby to wait for me. I quickly dress and run down, but he's not there either. I'm here all of one day, and my father is missing!! I'm frantic, and I don't know what to do or where to go first. He's a diabetic, and if he passes out or gets lost, he doesn't speak Italian. I step out in front of the hotel, and from blocks away, I see him walking toward me. He had walked all the way to the Coliseum alone. I'm amazed he knew his way back.

After taking in some sites with the group, we have a good amount of time to shop on our own. Dad finds a leather goods store steps away from the Trevi Fountain and is very pleased with his new purchase of a brown leather jacket. Like me, he has fallen in love with Michelangelo's Pieta' and eyes a bronze and marble replica at the vendor's stand a few feet away. It's very heavy, and he loves it so much, he wants to purchase four of them for our family. I hate saying no to him, explaining that we still have many places to visit before returning home, and each of them would need to be carried individually the entire trip. We can't possibly manage four of them and the luggage, too. I talk him into purchasing one large one for himself and three smaller ones for my sisters and me. He's not happy, but he accepts it. While on the tour bus one day, he looks at me and says, "When I go...... away, you know, you take the large Pieta'. I want you to have it." Tears well up in my eyes. He could not bring himself to say die, and I cannot deal with him even saying it. He's 78 now, has had diabetes for 16 years, and he doesn't eat right. He fights with me when I tell him not to eat ice cream or cake, but he's going to live life on his own terms regardless. Mom lived life on her own terms and passed at 59. I have to accept he'll never change.

When we arrived at the hotel in Rome, I asked if there's a refrigerator in the room for his insulin. They tell me we will have to refrigerate it in their bar. Two days later when we are ready to check out to begin our ride to Sorrento, the hotel manager informs me that the door to the bar is locked and that they'd have to MAIL the insulin to our next destination. Was he kidding? Wait for them to mail it? Not gonna happen! HIS father can wait for his insulin - not mine! I get on the bus and tell the guide we are not going anywhere without the insulin. Somehow, magically, they got the door open, and the bus is able to leave.

Sorrento is a vibrant resort town on the west coast of central Italy facing the Bay of Naples. There are always large crowds of people in the many restaurants no matter what time we pass them. The city is always alive. Many nights, Big Jerry would spend the evening with Dad on the terrace where there is usually an Italian singer, and most of the couples we are traveling with dance. It feels like I am watching a movie. Jerry's grandsons, the only young woman and man who are traveling with their parents, and I decide to go to an outdoor cafe. It's dark out, but the streets are lit by all the stores and restaurants and crowds of people living "*La Dole Vita.*" It is well after midnight when we decide to return to the hotel, and on the way back, we are all surprised when we pass a vendor selling hot food off his truck at this hour of the morning. The truck is triple the size of a hotdog vendor's, and we can't believe the amount of hot food he is selling. None of us can pass it up, and I order his sausage and peppers sandwich. Outstanding!

The following morning we take a ferry over to Capri. They give us a choice of going into the Blue Grotto or going to Anacapri; we can't do both. I tell Jerry and his grandsons that, as beautiful as the Blue Grotto is, I'd love for them to take the cable car ride over Anacapri. They agree, and the five of us go to the top of the island. We each get on the ride one at a time, and Dad's in front of me. The chairs are far apart from each other, and even if you yell, you cannot hear one another. Everything is going along smoothly, and from a distance, I can see Dad attempting to pick a piece of fruit from one of the trees as he's passing in the chair. I see him bending over, and if the bar against his stomach is not secure, Dad will fall - probably to his death.

Getting on the chair is not a big deal because there's someone there to help you on, but I hadn't given any thought about Dad getting off. No one from the ride is assigned to assist you at the end, but, fortunately, Jerry and the boys are in front of us, and when Dad's chair reaches the summit, they are there to catch him.

While departing for Sicily, Jerry finds out that his sister is hospitalized in Etna, which is close to Uncle Sal's family in Sperlinga. I tell the men of my uncle's history and what the town is like, and they, too, become infatuated. I rent a car, and the five of us drive to Etna before heading to Sperlinga. We walk into the hospital, and I immediately sense we've just walked into 1950. It's very cold in appearance, no bustling reception, no elevators, just cold concrete and stone walls. We find his sister's room that she is sharing with three other patients. There's a kitchen table in the room that they share, hot meals on porcelain dishes, and a centerpiece with fresh fruit. The patients are always well fed by both the hospital and their visiting families. Fortunately, the feeling of antiquity is no reflection on their care or the competence of their medical staff.

Driving from Etna to Sperlinga, we get lost for what seems to be hours, but the surrounding landscape is so stunning, none of us mind. Big Jerry is in the region where, except for him, his entire family has been born. It's so green and lush no matter where we look. We ride for miles and miles before coming to another village, finally arriving in Sperlinga. First, we go to the home of Uncle Sal's cousin, and the sign on the door tells us that he is not only the medical doctor in town, but he's also their dentist. We didn't have any phone numbers, so our trip is once again a surprise to them.

Dad and Jerry remain at the home of Uncle Sal's family while Jerry's grandsons and I are taken for a tour of the village by one of the young cousins. Unfortunately, she doesn't speak any English, and once again we go through the process of trying to communicate that we want to see Uncle Sal's cave. After some time, she understands, and when we arrive at the cave we came all this way to see, no one is home. We walk a little further, and a woman in a neighboring cave comes out to greet us. The boys are so anxious to get into see one of these homes, that when she invites us in for espresso, we accept without hesitation. It doesn't matter that none of us like espresso at all; we would agree to drink poison just to get inside.

As we enter her home, there is a large kitchen on the first floor and, of course, homemade pasta that's hanging on a long string spanning nearly the entire length of the room. Wood paneling covers the walls, and there's marble flooring and steps that continue up to the second and third floors. When we reach the third floor master bedroom, there is an enormous armoire on one side and a painting of the Madonna over the bed on the other. The only other decor on the wall is their wedding photo. If you step up to the door off the bedroom, you enter onto another street.

A few nights ago, the boys and I went to a dance club in Taormina overlooking the Ionian Sea called Toutva, French for "anything goes," that amazed us. There were several different bands dispersed throughout the large property, some indoors and some outdoors, all appealing to different genres. So when the neighbor invites us into the cave for espresso, Anthony picks up his cup and makes a toast, simply, "Toutva." The three of us laugh so hard, and I feel bad wondering if this very nice woman thinks we are making fun of her espresso. Certainly not.

We make plans for the following day to rent a car and drive to Sciacca, my paternal grandmother's birthplace. The only thing I know about Grandma is her name, and I realize that I had forgotten to take the date of her birth from her gravestone in New Jersey. I call Dad's sister, Aunt Katie, who doesn't know the year either, but agrees to go to the cemetery. We came all the way from the United States to find Grandma's home, and the only thing I forgot was the only thing I really need! Aunt Katie finds her birth year: 1881.

The following morning the five of us are back on the road toward Sciacca. It's a beautiful, large seaside city in the southwest corner of Sicily with exquisite views of the Mediterranean Sea. Aside from its position on the sea, Sciacca is best known for its thermal baths, which are among the best in the Mediterranean. As you would expect of a fishing port, the seafood is exceptional. The city is bustling, and we quickly see that getting a parking spot is our biggest challenge. We stop in front of a large, two-story picturesque building with a colonnade wrapping around the second floor and see that the cars are double and triple parked in the building's courtyard. Jerry turns his window down and asks a driver where the municipal building is, and the driver informs him it is the same picturesque building. By now, it's 10 minutes to 1, and if we don't get to the Hall of Records on the second floor before 1 o'clock, we must wait until siesta is over at 4. The driver then tells us that he is leaving and we can take his parking spot. It's as if Grandma herself is very much in control of us finding her home.

We quickly park the car and make a dash up to the second floor and down the colonnade. We make it within minutes, but I'm not confident that they will help us given that siesta begins in two minutes. The clerk speaks no English, and Jerry explains our situation. I don't know if it is the desperate look on my face, but she agrees to help. She searches and searches for the 1881 book of birth records and cannot find it. Now, I'm certain at this late hour we'll never get the address until, suddenly, she locates it. It's a long, ledger-sized book that contains the birth dates of every baby born in Sciacca chronologically. To add to the difficulty, we don't know what month Grandma was born, simply the year. She opens the book, and the once white pages are now yellow and are ripping as she's turning them a century later. She informs us that the only Francesca San Filippo born that year was on July 7th, and that the family lived on *San Filippo Cortile*. There is a gentleman standing next to Jerry telling us that he is heading in that direction and would walk us right to it. What were the odds we'd get a spot immediately in front of the building and now someone to walk us there? The clerk fills out a long paper, a new birth certificate of Grandma's that also contains her parents' and grandparents' names. She stamps a seal on it, and I nearly fall to my knees; it's so emotional. But there's no time for that; Jerry is yelling, "*andiamo, andiamo!*" as we are all following this stranger.

Walking out of the office, I keep blowing the clerk kisses, in lieu of words, so she knows how much I appreciate her help. We continue up the street toward Grandma's home, and Little Jerry, Anthony, and I run into a church along the way while Dad and Big Jerry are walking ahead with the gentleman. As we enter, the choir is practicing, and with the happenings of this afternoon, it's like the angels are singing for us. We continue up the block and make a left toward *San Filippo Cortile*. We reach the bottom of the *strata* to find that it's one of those narrow streets not suitable for automobiles. As we walk up the narrow road, two-story attached homes on both sides, women are looking out of their second floor windows and checking us out. As I pass each one, I can only say "*Ciao*," and they reply, "*Buongiorno*. " Jerry asks them in Italian if they knew the San Filippo family. How could they? They'd have to be about 150 years old to remember them. One woman actually said she knew of the family and remembered hearing they were very nice. Maybe that is true, and maybe she just said that to be nice. We'd never know. Either way, we have found what we came for. Actually, we don't know exactly which home on that street she lived in, but I feel close to my grandmother just knowing I was walking the steps she walked every day of her life until she left for America as a young girl. The church I had visited was probably where she was christened and where my family worshipped. I'm so elated, but I notice Dad is very quiet. Is he forgetting where we are? I ask, "Dad, do you know this is Grandma's block?" He replies, "Yeah, now what about my father?" Is he deliberately trying to kill me? I have no idea where Grandpa is from and neither does he. "Next visit, Dad; next visit, God willing." On our way out, we dine in the main piazza, and by now, we eat the same meal every day for lunch that Big Jerry has introduced us to, *Pasta alla Norma*, pasta with eggplant, famous in this part of Sicily and, of course, cannoli.

Little Jerry and Anthony keep teasing me, saying if I stayed married to Kevin and if their grandfather married my mother-in-law, I'd be their aunt now. The boys know how to make me laugh. Some nights it's just the five of us in some magical spot and we'll toast the night. We'll say what we are grateful for. It's incredibly sweet. But alone this evening and peering out into the night over the sea through my shutters in this stunning villa, I ask my grandmother quietly to send me someone to love. I tell her that I don't want to be alone when Dad leaves to join her in heaven and to please send me someone tall and dark with staggering good looks. Too much, Grandma?

Back in Taormina, Dad and I spend the afternoon shopping. I buy beautiful linens and two oil paintings that depict Grandma's street so I'll always have a piece of Sciacca. Dad doesn't really need anything, so he just tags along and is happy to just browse. Dad has been keeping up with me at every turn, and I'm always asking him if he wants to rest. When we see a bench outside one of the stores, we stop for him to take a break. He quickly falls asleep, so I decide to continue shopping. I won't be long, and he would know to wait for me. About 10 minutes pass, and I return outside only to find that he's no longer there. My heart drops. There are hundreds of people walking in both directions, how would I start to find him? The hotel is all the way down the hill on the beach, and with all the hotels, he would never remember which one. In a distance, I see him walking, and he's walking away from me. My hands are full, and I start running and screaming from the top of my lungs, "DAD, DAD, DAD!" I eventually get closer, and he hears me.

With little breath, I say, "Dad, where were you going? Did you think I would just leave you?"

He says, "I was going back to the hotel."

"But you don't know the name of it. How would you find it?" I ask frantically.

He puts his hand in his pocket and pulls out a key. He replies, "It's on the key. See, here."

Dad may have had little education, but he always had more common sense than anyone I know!

We head for our final destination, Palermo, and the guys and I are in our rental car where we'll meet the tour bus at our hotel, Villa Igliea. We drive for 1 1/2 hours until we reach the chaos of this big bustling city. It is 5 p.m. on a Friday afternoon, and the traffic here makes New York City feel like a remote village. It seems as if people are screaming all over the place, and then we realize it's probably because we are going down a one-way street the wrong way. The traffic in Rome is extremely noisy, but this is off the decibel meter. By the time we reach the hotel, I call the car company and inform them to come pick up their automobile because there's not a chance I'm moving another inch in this town. They're not surprised in the least.

This outstanding hotel is one of the most luxurious on the island, and it's hard to believe it was initially built as a private villa in the nineteenth century. It was restored at the end of that century and still has its original frescoes, decorations, and furniture. The villa has a magnificent position as it sits on the bank of the harbor. Exotic gardens surround the hotel, and the kidney-shaped pool hugs the edge of the property with the remains of the adjacent Roman columns on its edge, as if overseeing the yachts just feet below.

We are given the key to our room, the largest skeleton key I have ever seen. We walk up the stairs to the second floor, and I unlock the set of double doors to our room that are nearly 15 feet high. Once we enter through these doors, there is four feet of space before coming to an identical set of double doors, allowing for complete privacy. Our room is located overlooking the sea, and when we retire to bed, we can hear the tug boats all night long through the wooden shutters. It's like a dream!

It's our last evening of the tour, and I'm turning 40 tomorrow. A farewell dinner is prepared for our group on the patio. By now, everyone knows each other well, and the excitement of the trip culminates into an evening of joy and laughter. After dinner, the soprano singer in our group stands and leads the group into singing "Happy Birthday" to me. It's magical, me with Dad in Sicily on this special birthday in this amazing hotel.

The hotel has a grand piano on the patio, and there's an attractive female singer and a pianist performing tonight. She's singing mostly in English, a few Frank Sinatra songs done beautifully, and just before midnight she does "*My Way*." At the stroke of midnight, Big Jerry stands up, and I think he's announcing he's retiring to bed, but instead, he is just waiting for her to sing "Happy Birthday" to me. I can't remember a better birthday than this!

The following morning some of the hotel guests tell me that they heard her singing to me from their bedroom window. This is paradise, and, sadly, we're checking out.

*****

When we arrived in New Jersey, a friend picked us up at the airport and asked Dad how he enjoyed his vacation. Dad replied, "I like Florida better; at least they have dog races." Really, Dad! Dog races?! But I say nothing because I know how happy, content, and well taken care of he was over the last 15 days. He just really missed betting on some kind of race. Regardless, I was elated I was able to do this for us both. I've made a dream come true for him, and happily it involved Italy!

Once home, though, I was terribly sad every day. I got up every morning and worked at something I quickly learned to hate because I wouldn't lie to people about interest rates. I wouldn't lie about anything. I had no kids, no significant other, even though there were nice offers I rejected; no joy. To the outside world, I looked like I had it all, yet I couldn't fight the sadness, the depression, and I hated my life. All I thought about was returning to my happy place, Italy. Walking out my front door one day, I turned back and looked at my home, as if to peruse it, and asked myself, "What is this home missing?" I immediately knew the answer: It was missing a family.

A week later, I needed help fighting a sore throat. I parked in front of my doctor's office and began looking for a nickel for the parking meter, but found every coin except a nickel. As I crossed the street in the rain, I say out loud to myself, "There's a reason God didn't give me a nickel." Immediately I think why I would be blaming God? I was getting sicker. I ran into the doctor's office and asked the receptionist for a nickel. She didn't have one and called out to the only two people in the waiting room. One lady obliged, and when I returned, I went to hand her a dime, but she refused. A dime is not much, but I thought that was kind of a perfect stranger. I proceeded back to the receptionist's desk to sign in, and I see the name San Filippo as the last person registered. I ask, "Which one of you is a San Filippo?" It was the woman who gave me the nickel. I told her my grandmother was born a San Filippo and the story of my visit to her homeland. We discovered that we were, in fact, related through marriage. My mind started to reel. A former boss used to tell me that spirits work with coins. He would say that his mother dropped pennies for him to know she was around. I wondered if that was where the song *Pennies from Heaven* came from? If this was true, my mom would surely drop at least quarters. After all, she was a big spender, and I doubted she changed much even on the other side.

I was quiet as I sat there in the waiting room pondering what this all meant. Mrs. San Filippo was sitting across from me and couldn't see that my head was spinning. I attempted to look as if I was actually doing something and not just look like a vegetable sitting there, so I grabbed a magazine from the rack. There was no forethought into what I wanted to read; I merely picked one at random. I immediately opened it, not to the beginning, but somewhere in the middle. It's just where my finger stopped. The first word my eyes went to was "Sciacca!" At that moment, I knew Grandma was there and life would never be the same!

Chapter Four

FINDING FAMILY

Life at home: 2000

It been seven years since my last Italian trip, and Grandma's spirit continually visited me over the course of about a year. On several medical appointments, a San Filippo would be immediately in front of me. They were always in front of me, and they were always medical related. I came to believe Grandma was telling me she was there and that she was one step ahead of me. One of the most blatant, however, happened while sitting at an appointment in my office that I only agreed to because it was a referral. The man's last name turns out to be San Filippo. Not so strange ....until the switchboard operator tells me there's another man on the phone waiting to speak to me, also a referral. I agreed to take the call, once again only because of the referral, and his last name turned out to be Mancuso! My grandmother sent a San Filippo and a Mancuso at the same exact moment in time! What were the odds it wasn't her?

Dad has been living with me in my condo for the last four years due to a stroke he suffered on Mothers' Day 1996 that robbed him of all his short-term memory. The doctors said it was a minor one, but he doesn't know my sisters or me half the time, and he doesn't recognize his own home. The morning after the stroke, I walked into his hospital room, and the first thing he said to me was: "Where's Mommy?" Mom had been gone nearly eight years already. He lost at least that amount of time overnight. More than half his eyesight was gone, too, but he could comprehend what we were saying, and then he'd lose it in seconds. The day he moved into my home, he asked to see my birth certificate to prove who I was. Being so inundated with his needs and figuring out a way to make a living under these circumstances, I couldn't allow his condition to devastate me. I'd worry even more if he wasn't with me and imagine the worst. He's walking, talking, and eating very well, and I'm very grateful he's with me and not the Lord. All he keeps asking is, "Where is my mother?" Even after this head trauma, his devotion to her never waned. For the first two and a half years, I remind him each and every time that Grandma passed over 50 years ago, but after two years, I was forced to accept he was never going to get his memory back, and now when he asks about his mother, I tell him Grandma is coming tomorrow. He's very happy and less anxious, and I tell myself it's really not a lie because we'll all be reunited in the afterlife anyway. When I ask him if he wants me to put a sign on his bedroom door that reads "Ray's Room" because he can't remember which room is his, he looks at me and says in a sad and forceful way, "People won't think I'm crazy; they'll KNOW I'm crazy." While driving him to a medical appointment in hectic New York City, he's so confused, he looks at me and asks if we are on a mission. He thinks he's still in the Army and we're picking up an officer. My heart can't take anymore. He is my sick, adult child, and there is nothing I won't do to protect him - and he knows it. Before the stroke, I saw signs of memory loss, and several times we had a conversation as to whom he wanted to live with eventually. I naturally thought my siblings and I would share the responsibility given we did with Mom. Dad always said he'd prefer to live with me because I was the "most sensible" one, and he felt "safe" with me. There isn't a chance he is leaving me, especially when I hear from his roommate during his one-month rehab stay how my father was being mistreated by the staff. When things get so bad with the sleep deprivation and constant income worries, I think of Elie Wiesel and what he experienced with his father. Although his experiences were vastly different than mine, the feeling of protection and survival between parent and child is greatly understood. I've needed to remember that, unlike Elie Wiesel and his dad, we aren't in a concentration camp! I turn on Frank Sinatra, who is never further than a button away, and this simple act calms both Dad and me.

Dad can still easily climb the 27 stairs into my condo. Every Saturday night he dresses in his Sunday best, matching handkerchief, hat and all, and we go to Mass together. He may not remember who I am, but he can always recite *The Lord's Prayer* without hesitation. He loves every religious article. I'm a little surprised because he hadn't been a churchgoer all my life and realize this devotion is coming from his childhood. As we stand in line to receive communion, he reaches the priest, and when face to face with Fr. Peter, Dad places his hand on his shoulder and excitedly says, "How are you doing? I haven't seen you around." He says it as if he just ran into an old friend he hadn't seen in many years; meanwhile, he's only there to receive communion. Fr. Peter knows Dad well, and I can sense he's holding back from laughing. I take Dad's hand, and we return to our pew.

Today Dad and I are in line to approach the cross Father Ray is holding up. We are to kneel and kiss Jesus' feet on this occasion before we leave the church. As we approach the six-foot cross, Dad is confused, but eventually follows my lead and kneels and kisses His feet. Father Ray is so moved by Dad's mental state, he grabs Dad's head and kisses the top of it. This small gesture is so moving, as if Dad broke his heart. I take Dad's hand, and we move along.

My sisters and I stopped speaking, except through attorneys, soon after Dad suffered his stroke. Uninterested in helping with his care, they suggest we sell his home to pay for the help he needs, but the cost for a live-in is prohibitive, especially since all he needs is a babysitter. He merely needs family around. I refuse to throw away his hard earned savings. Even if I agree to sell his home, he will outlive the money, and then what? My sisters tell me to put him in a nursing home if I didn't want to sell, but that is never going to happen as long as I have a breath in me. To make things worse, one month before the stroke, I discovered large amounts of money taken from Dad's savings accounts, and Dad didn't understand what was happening. He just understood the money was gone. When I question my sister, I'm told, "It's none of your fucking business!"

To my sister's surprise, I take Dad to a meeting with his own attorney, whom he had never met previously and whom was hired by my sister, so she, too, could see his condition and as his attorney would certainly give an opinion. When the meeting ends, without even a question directed to her, Dad's attorney tells my sister that Dad wasn't as bad as she was led to believe and that he did not, in fact, belong in a home. So the enormous responsibility of his care, his home, his bad tenants, his expenses, all his legal issues, his medical care, etc., is all on me, and we're all alone now.

My relationship with that sister ceased to exist when I asked her to take him one weekend a month, and her response to me was: "He never did a fucking thing for me." From that moment, my blood ran cold towards her. Even when I wrote and asked her to mail me Dad's deed to his car because I needed to sell it for money, she sent a letter telling me I repulsed her and never to contact her again. She wanted "control" over both me and Dad, but she wanted to do relatively nothing for him. There would no longer be any dealings with her even though legally as co-executor with me she shared those responsibilities. Her hatred of me kept her away from her own father.......... Dad would never see her again.

Four years later, and Dad is still waking in the middle of the night and coming into my bedroom looking for his mother. It is as if I have had an infant in the house all these years. But it's harder, much harder! Once he collapsed in the shower from a drop in his blood sugar and I had to start showering him myself every day, I begin to call him by his first name, Ray, instead of Dad, having to call his name over a hundred times a day. Psychologically, it's easier for me to refer to him this way, as if in the third person, after seeing him nude. I can almost hear my mother saying Ray instead of me. I think how it should be her, not me, handling these problems, handling my sisters. My mind won't accept me bathing my own father, knowing he'll be devastated if he realizes who I am, and I'm afraid to find out how he'll react if he does.

At 6:30 a.m., the phone rings and the woman on the other end tells me what time the bus is coming to pick up Ray for the daycare center. I gently awaken him, help him out of bed, shower him, wash his hair, dry him off, blow his hair dry, powder his back because he loves it, lotion his legs and feet, dress him, test his blood, inject him with insulin, and then make him a big breakfast. The first time I gave him the injection, I cried. He looked at me and said, "It hurt you more than it hurt me." He gets a big breakfast: corn flakes with a whole banana, strawberries, and blueberries along with Carnations Instant Breakfast. When the horn blows, he's quick down the stairs to the bus. The people that run the center are very fond of him. They love his sense of humor and his natural good nature. On the day of his interview with them, he told the director he had been a bookie before retiring. She replied in a joking way, "I can report you, Ray." Laughing, he responded, "It's too late." Dad didn't remember his daughters any more, but he remembered the statute of limitations on booking numbers!

I lost my job in the mortgage business shortly after Dad became ill, as I could no longer keep the hours required. Yet, I stayed on as a volunteer with a homeless organization we, the volunteers, began a year before Ray took his stroke. I had a personal mission for years to help the homeless in light of the fact I was making a decent living providing home loans and felt I needed to give back. When our church announced a new mission to open a homeless shelter, I immediately jumped on board. We were sheltering, cooking, and counseling up to 14 people a day, the only facility that kept families together. We did it chiefly because of the kids. It was difficult and time consuming but also rewarding knowing the kids really needed this help. I'd even have some meetings at my own home to make it easier and cheaper than hiring another sitter when I was appointed to the board of directors the following year and served as treasurer.

Fortunately, I found another position working evenings and weekends selling educational software to young parents, and I hire senior citizens to babysit Ray while I work. For the first time in my professional career, I have to dress down for a job. I don't wear the nice suits, jewelry, high heels, or expensive bags anymore; I'm selling to a different crowd. I'm not supposed to look financially successful. I don't like the look on me, and after three decades of being a blonde, I become a vibrant redhead. My spirit may be free, but my body is not. More importantly, unlike nearly every commissioned salesperson in my field, I won't lie, and that always costs me business. Just asking for money is very uncomfortable for me. My dealings are always honest no matter how tight things ever get. It's remarkable I can make any kind of living.

I'm so stressed that I keep crying to God; I beg Him to take one of us; either one. If I'm gone, Ray will be taken care of with my assets. Either way, I've made sure he's not going in a nursing home.

With the sleep deprivation I endure every single day, I try to nap in the car between the three appointments each night. I have no social life, and my life is consumed with Dad's health and paying both our bills. My manager, Richard, is spending a good amount of time at my home in an attempt to get closer to me, and I don't mind because even though I have no feelings for him, he's a great help with Ray, and he sincerely cares about him, unlike most of the workers I pay. For this, I can overlook a lot. At the same time, the owner of the company, Preston, begins to get closer to me. He's tall, dark, and very handsome. Actually, he has staggering good looks and resembles Dean Martin so much so they could easily pass for brothers. I learn quickly that Preston was a professional Doo-Wop singer as a young man and was personal friends and sang for many years with Freddie Scott who had the big hit "Hey Girl" and Don & Juan who famously sang "What's Your Name?" Preston's not only handsome and gregarious, he's also extremely charismatic, a real showman. He continues to tell me that he's only been married two years to his second wife, also Sicilian, and how I'd enjoy meeting her. He tells me she recently turned 40 and how he wanted to take her to Sicily, specifically Palermo, for her birthday! Am I hearing things? I've asked my grandmother on MY 40th - in Palermo - for someone who is tall, dark, and possesses staggering good looks, and now there's one of them standing in front of me, but he's telling me how he wants to take HIS wife to Sicily for her 40th! Of all the things to tell me, he picks this?! How did this dream go so terribly wrong? What kind of sick joke is the universe playing on me?

Driving home one evening from a sales appointment, I phone the office as I did every workday and leave a message how I did that night. Did I make any sales? When the phone rings, Preston surprisingly answers. It was not unusual for him to be working in the evening when he'd typically be calling regarding a late payment. I give him the results of the day, and the conversation quickly turns personal. It's relatively late, and I've already worked TWO sales jobs, both on the road. I'll willingly give up either for one decent position! After such a tough sales call, I tell Preston how people are just plain nuts, and then I make the mistake of telling him I recently heard a bizarre story. I had no plans on saying anything more about it and realize immediately I probably said too much already. I am exhausted, and why I started this conversation escapes me. But Preston keeps pushing. I tell him it is just a story one of the day salesmen repeated to me, told to him by his girlfriend, that shocked me. I tell Preston I am too embarrassed to repeat it and how surprised I am that the guy even told me. I say that so he'll stop asking, but now he's even more interested, and I tell him I need to get off the phone because I'm driving. I make every attempt to get off the topic. The only people I've told this story to were two of my doctors. I wanted to hear what they thought; I was <u>that</u> curious. Both were stunned, given the expressions on their faces, but quickly had the same exact response: "That will work!" I never repeated it to anyone else.

I don't know why it's embarrassing to me; it's nothing I'm recommending. I just think it's over the top. I don't give in to Preston's probing, and then he says those magical words: "Want to stop by and smoke a joint with me?" I can't say yes fast enough. I know I'm going home to another night of bullshit from the senior helping with Ray and bitterly complaining that "Margery didn't rinse out the tuna cans." I've come to know why some men snap; they're married to women like her. I also know Ray will wake me up several times through the night looking for his mother. Do I want to smoke with you? I'll smoke with the devil tonight if he offers.

I enter the building and walk towards Preston's office. The moment he sees me, without even uttering hello, he anxiously says, " Tell me the story." I give in quickly because I know by now, without doubt, that he's not going to stop. I tell myself it's only something I'm repeating and I shouldn't feel so embarrassed. I proceed to tell him the story; I know a joint is forthcoming! I tell him that my coworker's girlfriend, a flight attendant, let him in on what is really happening in the friendly skies. She goes on to say that some of the male flight attendants are going into the restrooms during the flights and giving each other alcohol enemas. Why alcohol this way? So it's not detected on their breath.

Preston jerks back in disbelief and hesitates. Then he says, "What do they use? Champagne?" I laugh at the thought of using something carbonated. I visualize doing it with a six pack of beer and really laugh. I reply, "No, something like Vodka." I didn't give it any thought; it was just what came to my mind. Then he says, "Who would do something like that?" I respond - apparently without any thought - "Someone like me who doesn't like the taste of alcohol." The moment it comes out of my mouth I am sorry. His eyes nearly roll out of his head.

He wants to know exactly how this is being done. We both can't believe the story, and I keep telling him how we could never look at another flight attendant without wondering. He dismisses it in disbelief, but I tell him there are some of them that are, in fact, working under these conditions. He agrees. It's kind of frightening. What do you do if you're in flight and don't know if your attendant has been drinking? Do you ask to smell their ass? Are they inviting the pilots to do the same? Preston wants to know how they are actually performing this, what are the logistics, as if I have any idea. I can almost see his mind spinning out of control. With his dry, quick wit, you can never tell right away if he's serious or not. "Are they using tubes?" he wants to know. Tubes? Tubes?? I tell him they probably have disposable enema bags; that would make sense. He can't whip out a joint fast enough and ponder this excitement.

It would be a little while before I realized that he took my response to mean I liked the idea. Even though I had said I thought it was bizarre, when I answered him, "Someone like me who doesn't like the taste of alcohol," he took that to mean I thought it was a great idea. At that moment, my manager Richard walks in and we all smoke. Richard asks both of us if we want something from the deli, and I decline. I am looking down on my lap at the credit applications I'm finishing, and when Richard leaves the room, Preston says, "You want an olive with that?" I respond, "I'm not ordering anything from the deli." He says, "No, with your Drink!" It took me a moment to realize he was talking about the enema!

I am mortified and can only keep my head down, working on the applications. But my mind is buzzing; I am beyond mortified. At the same time, I thought it was hysterical. Preston keeps saying, "You're not answering me," but I continue to keep my head down out of embarrassment. I am pretending I can't hear him, but he knows I can. He couldn't say it any louder because Richard would overhear. After three attempts of getting my attention, Richard walks through the door, and the conversation is dropped.

It was from that moment I knew he wasn't going to leave me alone.............Wasn't going to happen!

After some time, I find that I am beginning to care for Preston far more than I should, and I know things are bad between him and his new wife already. He's sweet and kind, and I'm more than a little surprised how nice he treats the customers. He's genuinely nice to everyone, and my father is no exception. In all my years in sales, I've never known another salesman to be interested in any customer once they made their sale and got paid. Preston badly wants my friendship for a number of reasons, one being he likes me, likes my work, and he greatly respects what I am doing with my dad. He's been a caregiver to his own mother whom he continues to watch over. When I see him at the sales meetings every Friday, he craves my attention. His advances make my head spin as he expresses how he wished he had met me before getting married two years ago. I'm not there to carry on an affair with anyone; I'm just trying to keep Ray and me above water. But within two years, our relationship becomes physical. A few short months after that, I end it. I didn't want it for myself. But I fell in love with him from the first "olive request." I desperately need a break.

A check arrives from a former employer I worked for decades ago stating they were forwarding me money left in an old retirement account they would no longer be servicing. At the same time, a former boss asks me to help him out short-term, and I agree. One day I ask him what he did with all the points he accumulated on his credit card, and he says nothing. Within a few days, I am booking my flight to Italy with his points and using the retirement funds that came from nowhere. Another power was making it possible for me to take that much needed break. Jeanne is happily married to her third husband, and Debbie has no interest in returning to Italy anytime soon, so it's me going it alone. I don't mind at all because I will be able to do anything I want like try and locate my family in the southern region and go horseback riding often. I'll fulfill my childhood dream of being able to saddle up at any time. I am not nearly as skilled as my cousins who grew up with horses and who would occasionally invite me to join them. I'd learn to ride in the saddle, no lessons. But I have guts, and that's what I'll pack.

My friends and the family I have left in my life aren't surprised at all. They know how happy I am in Italy; they see the excitement in my face just talking about it. Not knowing the language and driving that much all alone frightens them, but, to me, I feel like I'm among cousins I've just never met when I'm there. I think the worse that would happen is I'd get my ass pinched by some stranger. My excitement overshadows any logic. Dad's brother, Uncle Leo, will sleep at my home and oversee his needs. Even short-term, there will be no nursing home for him.

I fax Cesare and tell him I'm returning to Italy and plan to locate my mom's family in the Salerno region. When I realized my paternal grandmother's spirit was with me in 1993 and attributed this connection to the fact that I went to her grave, I visited my mother's family gravesite and prayed to them in the hopes they'd assist me in finding their family in Italy. When I turned and started to walk away from their headstone, their bodies directly below me, I get the distinct feeling at that moment that they are trying to tell me something - as strongly as if they were standing there. I pivot and turn back, staring at the headstone, and I "know" it has something to do with their name. I have no idea what this means, and I say aloud, "If you want me to find your family, then please send me the address; you have more power than I do." Am I losing my mind? Doesn't feel that way! But my friends definitely think so.

I drive past the large wrought iron fence out of the cemetery, and I think about my Great Aunt Lizzie that lives nearby and that maybe I should stop in to pay my respects in Mom's absence. She is elated to receive company. She lives in a three story walk-up, and rarely does anyone just drop by. I stay long enough to have coffee, and as I get up to leave, she asks if I want to look at some old photographs. I know they're family pictures I've never seen before, and I'm anxious to see them. She takes out an old cookie tin, the kind you put your homemade sugar Christmas cookies in. There seems to be hundreds of photos in this one tin alone. We look at the first few, and she quickly removes the only piece of paper in the tin, shoving it in my face and continually saying, "This is Grandma's address in Italy; this is where she's from." It's merely 30 minutes after I left the cemetery where I asked the spirits for it, and miraculously it's in my face! Who's nuts now?

I write to the address Aunt Lizzie hands me and explain who I am. A few months pass, and I receive a phone call from a woman living in the same city I reside telling me she was visiting her family in Sant' Arsenio, Italy, when their next door neighbor received my letter. She carried a letter back to me from my cousin and told me how happy she was to receive mine. It was the first contact anyone had with our Italian relatives in probably 100 years.

Seven years have passed since I received this letter from my Italian cousin, and I give Cesare my cousin's name and address, and his secretary is able to locate a phone number. They try for days, but there's no answer; it just keeps ringing. My mind tells me if it's ringing, there's life at the other end. I book a room for two nights in the Salerno region to go in search of *la mia famiglia*, my family.

***

I arrive in Rome, and it is electrified more than usual because it's the year of the Great Jubilee. I'm disappointed Cesare is out of town on business. He's one of the most interesting people I've ever met. I stay a few nights and do my normal shopping for leather bags and shoes, and walk to my favorite sites before heading south to find Great Grandmother Cappola's family.

I see the signs for my hotel and climb the very narrow road in the dark to their parking lot that appears to be on a cliff. The road is so narrow that I scratch the side mirror on my rental. After checking in, I tell the receptionist why I'm there, and she quickly offers to help in my quest. I'm elated as she opens a phone book and sees a number of someone on the same street as my cousin and immediately dials the phone. The woman on the other end tells her that she does, in fact, know my cousin and that she is staying with her daughter Maria in Polla a few towns away. The woman gives her Maria's last name, and we're able to get her phone number, too. The receptionist phones and tells Maria that there is a relative from the United States looking for the family and that I don't speak Italian. I'm instructed to drive to Polla the following day and look for the area marked "piano." She says there's a bar there, and across the street from the bar is a shoe store. There's someone there that speaks English, and I should ask them to call her. I cannot help but wonder how difficult it is going to be to locate this shoe store, but I've come this far, and I'm determined to meet my family. At home, I travel to three appointments each night, mostly in the dark with my 14-year-old BMW, and have to constantly stop to look at my paper map. I know that if I am capable of getting to these insane business appointments, I can find my way around Italy and locate my family.

Anxiously tossing and turning, I hardly sleep that night and make my way to Polla the following day. I find the "piano" area and pass the bar with about six guys just hanging outside of its front door. I find parking, but I am forced to walk past the bar with the guys still there. As I'm passing them, they just look, and I nod. No brash cat calls, at least none that I can hear, and I'm grateful for that. I see the shoe store and cross the street anxiously. I walk in and start to explain why I'm there but quickly find out that there's no one there that speaks English! How did this one very important detail get so lost in translation?

But the Italians help each other. I walk back to the bar with all the guys still outside and ask if anyone speak English. Typically, I find someone who speaks English every third try. Sure enough, someone takes me into the bar and telephones my cousin. Within a few minutes, a car arrives, and we're driving up to the top of the mountain to her home. As I walk into the living room, I am greeted with trepidation. I sense their tension, and fortunately I thought of bringing the letter I received from them seven years earlier. When I hand it to them, their apprehension fades away, and I am suddenly no longer a stranger but a beloved relative returning to the roots of her great grandmother. *La Famiglia* - what a beautiful adventure!

A few minutes pass, and it quickly becomes awkward because we cannot communicate with each other. Then a woman walks through the door, and I immediately ask her if she speaks English. She replies, "I hope so; I was born in the Bronx." I tell her of the memory I have of my great grandmother, how beloved she was, and how during this trip I wanted to meet my family. I tell her I'm interested in seeing where my great grandmother was actually born. She translates for us, and within minutes we are all in the car driving to Sant' Arsenio. Walking with Maria and her mom

91

through the piazza, me in the middle, they wrap their arms around my waist as if to show me off. As we continue down the *strada*, people are yelling, "*Ciao, Maria. Come stai*"? Everyone knows everyone. I'm elated and proud. Against all odds, I found my family!

We continue by walking through the main piazza, stop in to see the church where Grandma worshipped, and then proceed to the home she actually lived in. I'm stunned to find out that the home was still in the family. My cousin's parents lived in it, and I immediately feel Maria's sense of love for the home. The Italians are not like the Americans in that regard. They have a home, and that's typically where they stay until their death, or in this case, until they left for America. No one lives in the home, but the rooms are still furnished and covered with white sheets. Maria takes a vase from a shelf in the kitchen, places fresh cut flowers in it, and places it on the kitchen table. I don't ask why; I can only assume she senses the spirits will see them. Even after death, we want to make our parents happy.

We ride back to Polla, and Maria's adult children are home from work. They set the dining room table and prepare a great spaghetti and meatball dinner. Even without being able to communicate with each other, I feel their love, and when my cousin puts her arm around my waist for the photos, I feel my grandmother's arm around me. It's now dark, and I need to return to my hotel an hour away. They beg me to stay the night, but I explain that I have a very long drive the following day to Tuscany and that my hotel is in that direction. They even want to follow me to the hotel so they know I arrive safely, but it's too far, and I promise to telephone when I arrive. Walking out, Maria hands me a lace doily she crocheted herself and a box of chocolates to remember them. The chocolate won't last the trip to Tuscany, but the doily will be with me forever.

The following morning I begin my six-hour drive north to Tuscany. I've never been there before, but certainly heard of its beauty. I've come here now to live on a farm and be among the vineyards! I found a woman online that specializes in Italian vacations who has been assisting me with booking a place to stay for the week. I don't want to stay in a hotel and decide on a farmhouse, an *agriturismo*. I find it fascinating that it's even a choice I have. I've read "*Under The Tuscan Sun*," and like everyone else who read it, I want to visit Cortona. My broker tells me of a great family that runs a nearby farm and has a restaurant on the property. Given I am alone, she recommends this place out of all the other choices even though it is a little out of the way.

It is nearly four hours before I reach the bottom of Tuscany and see my first cypress tree. You cannot think of Tuscany without thinking of these magnificent trees symbolic of the Tuscan landscape. They can survive for up to 2,000 years reaching 80 feet, and the Etruscans believed them to have supernatural connections. Driving by the villas, they line the driveways on both sides, sometimes passing hundreds of them before reaching the main house. The Tuscans also plant them on the borders of their property to mark their property lines. To say they add beauty is an understatement.

My car is climbing the mountain as I pass Cortona in search of San Pietro a Dame to find Agriturismo Acquaviva. The road is getting narrower and narrower as I'm winding around the edge of the mountain for 22 minutes to the top of the mountain and Acquaviva. As I make the very sharp left turn into the driveway, I'm greeted by all the neighboring dogs, some barking loudly and others just sniffing me out. There are two large homes on the property within 200 feet of each other and two in-ground swimming pools near each. Three smaller homes are scattered throughout the property with a large, one-story, industrial looking building in the distance that house the farm's pigs. These are no ordinary pigs; they are the biggest pigs I have ever seen in my life.

The noise from the dogs sounds the owners that someone has arrived. Angelo and Maria come to greet me and neither speak English, but their reception is warm and inviting, and I immediately feel at home. They assist with my luggage and show me to the small, two-story, stone building on the left close to the street and overlooking the valley. There's a staircase next to the driveway to my second floor bedroom where Angelo carries up the luggage. The front door has hanging ropes that cover it top to bottom, allowing fresh air into the room but keeping flies out. The building was originally used for farm animals hundreds of years ago, and then when Italy allowed farmhouses to be used as vacation homes, *agriturismi*, many of these structures were converted all over the country. As you enter through the ropes, there's a kitchen with one window over the sink that overlooks the valley and a large fireplace that heats the apartment. Next to that in the corner is the tiniest spiral staircase leading to the second floor. As you wrap your body around the staircase, you enter the bedroom with new terra cotta flooring and en suite bathroom. There's double doors that lead out to a staircase, a window on the adjacent wall, and another window in the bathroom with an incredible view of the valley below. From here, I can hear the sheep's cow bell when they're returning home from the valley.

Behind my apartment is a canopied area where the three horses are tied at night. No stables; just the canopy top. During the day, the horses roam the village at will and return at dinnertime. I make it known when I meet one of their three grown children that speaks a little English that I'm there to ride whenever they're available. He has a very familiar face to me, someone American, but I cannot figure out who. His skin coloring, hair, shape of forehead and jaw are very recognizable to me, but I cannot place who it is no matter how much I stare. I cannot understand what they are saying to each other, but I can tell he is arguing with his dad that he wants to be the one riding out with me. I don't care; I just want to ride.

I bring my Italian dictionary with me everywhere. Hopefully I'll learn more than *"come sta"* and *"vaffanculo."* I know nearly nothing, and I'll need to communicate with them if they are providing my room and food. Maria is wonderful and is always laughing. I find out that she not only has the job of taking care of the sheep on the farm, but she's the main cook at the restaurant AND a full-time school teacher in Cortona! I don't know how this woman has time to smile, never mind be happy! I'm convinced she has the answer to life.

Angelo comes into the restaurant after he's finished his chores and changes his clothing. He's not allowed in after working in the pigs' pen otherwise. I try walking up to see what a pigs' pen looks like, but I get within about two blocks and have to turn around because of the stench. Two friggin blocks! The entire family eats together in the restaurant each night after serving the customers, and they are all always happy and laughing. The food is incredible, and the patrons love Maria.

The following morning I am putting my make-up on by the bathroom window, and I see Maria's son looking for me to go horseback riding. I yell down, *"Cinque minuti,"* and five minutes later we are saddling up with Western saddles, odd for Italy, as most are English. I'm able to communicate that I want a horse that likes to run, and a few minutes later Maria's son and I are riding off. It's a gorgeous day, and soon we cross over into Umbria. I'm in heaven as we ride through woods and dirt roads, passing through tiny villages. It's a mixture of small farms, *agriturismi*, and residential homes. All have olive trees. There are less cypresses here and far fewer vineyards the nearer we are to the Umbria border. Many have horses, and most have dogs. Many of the dogs run freely in the community and hang out together. They are fun to watch but not always fun to hear. We're riding so close to some of the front doors, I think I can ring a doorbell without getting off my horse. We make our way back home, and as I go to dismount with his help, I feel his hand on my butt, and then his hand reaches between my legs and cups my most private part. I'm in disbelief; I'm his mother's age! As I reach the ground, I'm stunned, and my first thought is that it was an accident. My second thought is it was no accident, but I literally don't have the words to say anything. I didn't acknowledge it in any way because I was embarrassed ..... for him. It's at that moment I realize who he looks like - my ex-husband! I could not see past his farm clothes and long hair to see the resemblance until now. I'm divorced so long I don't remember my ex's face!

I eat at the farm nearly every night, and Maria makes me feel like family. I'm surprised to find out that the restaurant is the building immediately next to my apartment. It's so close, I can almost treat it as a drive-thru - but better, much, much better! On the outside, it appears to be just another stone structure, but once inside, there's more than one dining room. The tables are covered with white linens, fine china, stemware, and fresh cut flowers. At the end of the room, there's a large bar where one of her sons is usually making espresso or pouring wine or a complimentary cordial.

Maria shows me a menu that she is preparing for her restaurant and asks me to help her translate it into English. Using my pocket dictionary, I'm able to translate all except one. I understand it's from a pig, but I don't know what it's called. She's tapping her butt as if to say it's from the pig's behind, but I know nothing about pigs and their meat. After some time, I say in English, "Write pig's ass." I thought she would never find the humor as my mother would, but she roars in laughter. Everyone in the restaurant wants to know what she is laughing about, and she continues to howl as she repeats what I said in Italian. As it turns out, the word is prosciutto, and she has the best I have ever tasted! Home-grown prosciutto. Who would have thought?

I drive down the mountain daily to visit and get lost in all the towns I have mapped out in the region. Each day I notice more and more the poppies that are appearing all over the landscape, nearly the first to officially notify you that Spring has arrived, those tiny, red, glorious momentos of God saying hello. If I pick one, it will die almost immediately, but if I just leave it alone, it will stay all Spring long. I'm told that the most scenic drive in the Chianti region is between Siena and Florence. I drive three hours to visit Siena and spend a stunning afternoon there. It's very difficult breaking away from this incredible city where I love people watching and sipping cappuccino in their main piazza, the location of the famous Palio horserace. But I'm set on driving the Chianti route up 222. By the time I reach the bottom of the route, it's already dusk, and I've only just begun. I am amazed at the stunning beauty of the "*dolci colline,*" rolling hills that are surrounding me at every turn, as if God himself took a brush and painted the land with grape vineyards and olive groves sitting side by side - and then created it. To compliment the landscape, large, outstanding villas are perched on top of each hill overseeing their land. Up the winding road through the small, quaint villages, I ride not wanting to miss one vineyard. I go nearly as far as Florence and turn around to go back to Maria's, about a four-hour drive. I'm accustomed to driving for hours each night at home in the dark, not knowing how to reach my three appointments and constantly stopping to read my paper map, but today I'm driving through heaven. It's Frank Sinatra and me alone, and I'm in my glory. I notice a beautiful villa from the road named Casa Frassi that has a restaurant and decide to stop for dinner. I meet a young woman, also dining alone, from the United States and invite her to sit with me. Over dessert, she informs me that the gasoline strike has begun already, a few days earlier than had previously been reported. To say it's a stressful ride home is an understatement. I pass many gas stations, and not one of them is open. I decide to go forward and take my chances because I have nothing with me except my pocketbook, and if I reach Cortona and think I cannot make it up the mountain, I'll take a room there. The strike is expected to last for several days.

I drive slow with the idea it will conserve gasoline, and for what seems like days later, I'm able to reach Cortona. I know I should take a room, but having no other clothing or anything else, I take the risk and climb the mountain. I'm so frightened as I make each turn. If I run out of gas, will the next car be able to stop before hitting me? I don't know if the lights on the car would even be lit in that case. I know I'm taking a big risk.

I cannot believe when I arrive San Pietro a Dame without incident. An angel had to have been pushing my car. I cannot venture out the next two days, and when Angelo reassures me that the strike is over, I literally roll my car all the way down the mountain to a station.

With a gassed up automobile, I say my good-byes. Maria's son never approaches me the remainder of the week other than to be cordial or bring me a cappuccino, and I pretend like nothing happened. I never want his mom to know. And I know I'll return some day; I just don't know when. With Ray, I know even less. Still, I wouldn't trade my life with Dad for anything. My dream is to have a second home and a couple of horses here, and Dad is always there in the dream. He doesn't ride with me, but he is there to send us off like Ben Cartwright did with his sons. As I make that 22-minute drive down the mountain, I sob all the way. I know

I'm always going to cry when I leave Rome, but when I leave Tuscany, I sob.

I reach the bottom of the mountain and arrive Cortona when I see an old woman seemingly struggling to walk up the hill and carrying fresh cut flowers. It's getting hotter outside, and I think how dangerous it could be for a senior. I stop and ask if she needs a lift, and not understanding each other, she gets into my car anyway. I'm shocked she had the guts to get into a stranger's automobile, but I'm happy, too, that she did. I follow her directions and think I'll be driving her home and just maybe she'll invite me in for a cup of cappuccino. I'm really interested in seeing how an old villager lives here. Will it be anything like I've seen in the Italian movies? My anticipation is building as I make the turns she's pointing out, and then I realize where she was walking to - her husband's grave! I let her off in the cemetery, and she's so grateful she hands me a flower, one of the ones she picked for her husband. She gets out of the car, and there is no way I can ask her if she wants me to wait and drive her home. I can feel her gratitude as she grabs my hand good-bye. As she's walking away, I begin to really sob. Too many good-byes for one day.

Then I remember, I'm getting to hug my dad today!

***

I returned home to the same scenario. Dad was still doing well, eating healthy, and he was happy and gregarious nearly all the time. Most importantly, I saw no real difference in his mental capacity such as Alzheimer's that the doctors said he probably had. He continued to look for his mother constantly. There was no contact with my siblings, and I continued to receive no help or money from any family member. Money worries consumed me.

Within a few months of Father Ray grabbing Dad at the altar and kissing the top of his head, I received the shocking news of Father Ray's passing. Dad would attend his wake dressed in his Sunday best. Dad understood what his presence was about; he just didn't remember who the person was in the coffin. Dad never spoke about his own passing except to say he didn't want to live if he became a burden. I never got the impression he was afraid of death, but he wanted to live to 100 so he would hear the weatherman announce it on morning television.

I was still working for Preston while I continued to look for another sales position. Over time, I saw his life was spinning out of control. I liked his new wife when we first met until I learned that all she wanted to do was party like an 18-year old on drugs. What disgusted me the most was that she was a mom herself with a 16-year old boy. And she loved her cocaine, too. Preston did it occasionally until he married her, then it was all the time. Ironically (or sadly), they met not long after he suffered a heart attack, and yet, she was still promoting cocaine for them both! He still wanted my attention, but he was never going to get my approval. Our relationship became such that the only way I would meet with him to discuss business was in a diner, out of the eyes and ears of the undesirables, the riff raff that was now walking through the office, and our relationship became more and more contentious. But in those less than contentious moments, he'd always ask the same thing: "Have you tried the enema yet?" I always laughed and said no and would ask him if he tried it yet. Always to my surprise, he'd say no. He'd say he was waiting for me! I always laughed, but I was hurting inside. I walked away expecting to hear the worst possible news of him one day, and I didn't think it was far off. My heart was broken.

Chapter Five

GOD MADE NOCTURNAL ROOSTERS?

Life at home: 2002

Ray and I move back to his home because he could no longer make the stairs in my condo, and I need to be a resident to evict his tenants after the wife assaulted me. Not only do I have legal problems with my own family, now I have a legal issue involving Dad's home that needs to be handled immediately. I'm under attack on every front. Dad continues asking for his mother, but he sleeps mostly through the night since he started wearing diapers. Fortunately, he's typically happy and still looks 15 years younger than he actually is. I'm so proud of him. His good humor and big smile flashing those pearly whites are the same, and he continues to love company, any company. He prefers that they bring their children along, too. All the kids love him and want to push him in his wheelchair. They become fast friends. He cannot walk much, but he can easily stand while showering every morning. His appetite is excellent, and above all, he feels safe. When he's ready for bed, I kiss him good-night and ask if he saw his mother today. He usually says he didn't see her but he did speak to her. His language is diminishing each passing day, but he's still smiling and eating.

Moving back to Dad's home is the last thing I want to do. Life has been so difficult for the past six years, and moving means not only will Ray no longer attend the adult daycare center, but I'm also losing the seniors I hired as his "babysitters." The seniors said they'd drive to our new home, but they are very unreliable already. All these years, when they called in sick or wouldn't drive over because there was a dust of snow on the ground, I couldn't go to work, and I work solely on commission. The only break I catch is when Dad's other tenants switch homes with us, and I'm spared the problem of finding new tenants for my home. Cousin Joe, who had been living in the basement, was moved to the top floor after the eviction.

Financially, things have changed, too. I've recently discovered we can now do a reverse mortgage on a two-family home. Being able to use the equity in the house to pay for his growing needs as he deteriorates is a tremendous gift; a tremendous peace of mind! The first thing I buy is a 61" television so Ray is able to see it with his impaired vision. He won't be able to miss it. He's blind on the left side in both his eyes; he cannot even see the food on the left side of his plate. When Marie Barone on *Everyone Loves Raymond* walks through the door and asks her son Ray if he wants lasagna, Dad yells excitedly, "Yes, I want some." The television is that large. I understand what this mortgage means to his assets, but I also know his equity will now outlive him. It's all for him; the way it should be. The best part now is I never have to leave him and go to work because for the first time I have rental income of my own. There would be a gift for us, too, when we returned home and meet our new caregiver, Rose! We love her like family - loving family! Of ALL the seniors I hired over the years, Rose would turn out to be the only sincere one.

I haven't spoken to my siblings in years regardless of the fact one of them is on the Power of Attorney with me. I should be getting my own attorney, and at this point, Dad will probably be gone by the time we'd get to court. I'm overwhelmed every single day, but, still, it's never a consideration he's going to leave me either. I handle each day as things come up because that's the way it's thrown at me.

On 9/11, I, like everyone else, heard the horrific news of the Twin Towers falling. Knowing my youngest sister worked about a block from the towers, I called her home, and I was happy to hear her voice. I could have hung up without her ever knowing who it was, but I spontaneously took the opportunity to go forward. I told her how worried I was about her, and she told me that she had called in sick that day. What were the chances? I went further to say that I loved her and that there was something I had found out that she should know because, being the youngest, it affected her the most: Daddy had a stroke when she was a young girl, and that was the reason for his personality change. He began to hate people in the family that he never had ill feelings for, he became even more frugal to the point it was abusive to my mother while she was sick, and he had no compassion for my sister's financial hardship going to school. He became paranoid about people for no logical reason. I tell her that he had kept it from all of us, even Mommy, not to worry us. It was well known in the family that Dad always worried about suffering a stroke like his cousin, and Dad always said he would rather be dead than live like that. He's said it many times. Mom, however, was different. She didn't want to go no matter how much of a burden she was. It was total fear of the unknown. To find out Dad had actually suffered in silence was heartbreaking to me. I naively thought that when my sister heard that he had a medical reason for his change in behavior, she would actually change her attitude toward him. Dad wasn't trying to deprive her of anything, nor did he ever raise a hand to any one of us. I thought the truth would have changed her heart. But all she did was thank me for saying that, and when I asked if we could get together and see the baby, she said she'd phone me. She never called.

The work with the homeless continues. I am attending meetings, paying their bills, completing paperwork for grants, and I hear the stories of the people we have taken in, our "guests." The stories are upsetting to me, to say the least. Some of these people repulse me. I can't make these stories up. One of the fathers and his two teenage sons won't even bathe, and the other guests are complaining of the stench. We were also notified that another family was going door to door and asking if their young child could use their bathroom. Once inside, the child was taught to steal. But I do it for the kids, the ones that don't steal. We are helping them with homework and bringing in games. They get to see firsthand people helping people. For me, I wanted the kids to know this is what Jesus preached, helping the less fortunate without making them feel that way. They are adequately fed by us, but I see that even though food is provided by the parishioners of the eight churches that are supporting this mission, many of the guests consistently have food delivered to them by local restaurants when their welfare checks arrive. They all have the same mentality and think only of today.

I wonder if all the good we are doing, attempting to do, is really worth it. Are any of them decent human beings? If so, they are hard to find. There is a reason they are homeless, and it's normally not just unfortunate luck. For the most part, they just don't want to work, and they all know how to work the system; their families have been doing it for generations. It is easier to take from the system than to work. But we do it for the kids; it is always for the kids.

An old friend telephones me after three decades and leaves a message telling me she needs a friend and remembered what a good one I was to her all those years ago. We had worked together, literally three feet apart, and we socialized out of the office a few nights a week until she married and went on to

105

have five kids. After that, we no longer had much in common until 30 years later when her mom became stricken with Alzheimer's, and she, too, became her parent's caregiver. I thought I knew everything about Angela until I returned her call and her husband mentioned something about her "other" mother. There's ANOTHER mother? He proceeded to tell me that when Angela's father suddenly passed when she was just 13 years old she had to be told the truth about her parents. Her dad had connections to Al Capone (I remembered the family was originally from Chicago, so that made sense) and, not surprising at all, he had a mistress as well. His wife was unable to conceive, but his mistress had no trouble in that department. He went on to have four children with his mistress, and after giving birth to the last one, Angela, the mistress allowed him to take all of them and be raised by his wife. They told Angela at the time of his sudden death so that she could be legally adopted by the woman she knew as her mother, the only child still under 18. But Angela never spoke of it; Mom was Mom and that was it........... That is... until now.

Angela's mother is in the last stages of Alzheimer's and is non communicative. The last time she spoke a word was years ago on Christmas Day at the dinner table when she picked her head up and said, "I love you, Angela." Everyone there was hysterically crying. That was the only Christmas gift Angela needed; the one from God. She'd never speak again. Like me, Angela wasn't going to leave her in a home until recently when she needed to be hospitalized and couldn't be taken off machines. With her mother in the nursing home now, Angela wants another change. She wants out of her marriage of 25 years. She just landed her first real job and is looking for a small place to live. As it happens, Dad has a finished basement, and I certainly would welcome her being there with us. Who better than another caregiver? Someone compassionate, and not like the phonies I pay to babysit him.

For both Angela and me, this reunion is heaven sent. We plan on moving in on the same day, June 1st.

The day of the move couldn't be more difficult when the senior, who is scheduled to stay with Dad, calls in sick. Then, to our disbelief, Angela phones telling me that her mother passed that very morning - the very same day Angela is making a big change in her life. We both feel it is her mom's way of saying they should both move forward. Oddly, Angela had recently given her mom the heartfelt permission to let go as well.

It's been a year since I left Preston's employment. I never wanted to get physically involved with him; I was dead set against it. I was able to keep him and his advances at arm's length, despite the attraction, until he pulled out his joint - and I don't mean the one in his pants! The marijuana had everything to do with giving me more patience and tolerance with my mentally disabled father, and Preston had it. It wasn't just good for me, it was good for Dad because I could remain calm even after asking me a hundred times that day where his mother is! Everyone is happier as the stress lifts from me. It isn't like my mom's old drug, Valium, she swallowed when she became overwhelmed or the antidepressant I took and waited for three months to help me that never worked. With the marijuana, the relief is immediate! My doctor says he would prescribe marijuana for me if he could because he's known me for decades and knows how responsible I am; he knows my life, and he knows the help it gives me. All the same, it's not legal.

The only one who ever knew about my short affair with Preston was Angela. I kept it from Jeanne because she was suffering greatly as a result of her cheating husband. I couldn't justify it to myself; I always knew it was very wrong. I gave my resignation to Richard and never even said good-bye to Preston. For MY sake, it had to end this way, and I needed to get him completely out of my life. I found another sales job working evenings in the field again selling prime meats.

Angela reminds me that decades before I always talked about us going to Italy together, and now she wants to go. When I phone the county about getting in-home assistance for Ray, I am told that all their funds were already allocated. Angela begins making vacation plans, even asking her boss for time off, and I keep telling her that it would take a miracle to get help. I think she's crazy. Like we're really going to get a miracle.

The very next morning I get that miracle! The county calls and tells me they were giving me someone for the days I need! We know it had to be Angela's mom pulling the strings from above. Now who's crazy? No coincidence, I think.

My oldest friend, Jeanne, is turning 50 and recently separated from her third husband against her will. It has been 28 years since we made our last trip to Italy together, and this time, I know much more - I know to bring a sweater when I cross the Alps. Jeanne and Angela are acquainted with each other through me, both are easy going, and both trust my decisions on planning the entire trip. The three of us will go to Italy, and once again, I'll be the guide.

I talk nonstop about Casa Frassi, how it sits on *Strada* 222, the most magnificent stretch of land in the Chianti region and only 15 minutes from Siena, my favorite Tuscan city. We'll get an apartment on this vineyard. I don't know the cost and I almost don't care. Whatever it is, the three of us will split it. It's all I can think about, a week on this incredible vineyard. I email the hotel and inquire as to which apartments are available. With a full apartment, we'll be able to cook our own meals most of the nights. But when I get my reply, they inform me there are none available for that week. I refuse to accept no. So I write back and plead my situation of being a caregiver, how I need this vacation, how I found them passing by, etc. They must have taken pity on me because suddenly an apartment became available. I am elated!

***

Touching down in Rome, we immediately make the three-and-a-half hour drive north to Casa Frassi. From 222, you can see the imposing main building made of white stone, the same one that drew me in driving by two years earlier. As we make our way through the long, winding driveway lined with cypresses, Angela and Jeanne, too, are struck by the beauty of our surroundings. The vineyards are in full bloom with the lush, large green vines that intertwine for what looks like miles while their purple Sangiovese grapes hang heavy off the vines. It looks like a postcard. The vineyard is beginning the first stage of turning grapes into wine this week. Harvest started over a week ago, but there's still an overabundance of grapes waiting to be picked.

We spend a week visiting many small villages in addition to Siena and Florence where we'd window shop on the Ponte Vecchio and pay over $7.00 for a can of Coke. Even here, I'm always thinking of Dad and worrying, but I tell myself I have so many people stopping by and checking on him like his sister Katie, Rose, and my old friend Joe, a cop in town, that I reassure myself. And my traveling friends have their own problems that are just as serious to them. Both are going through contentious divorces, and all of Angela's five grown children are against her. As it turns out, all three of us are going through tremendous changes in our lives at the same time. This vacation is a dream come true!

I know Dad can't live forever, and I don't know how to live without him. I begin to think about moving here when he's gone, but I don't know what I'd do especially given the fact I don't speak Italian. We make reservations for a wine tasting on a vineyard that has about 25 Arabian horses just playfully roaming the grounds. We're told that the horses are a passion of the owner and that they are merely there as pets. They also tell us that the workers are allowed to ride them at will. After a tour of the property, the hostess takes us into the wine cellar where we have a tasting of several of their own wines. She works only when people make a reservation for the tour, and a room on the property is provided for her. This sounds perfect for me when Dad's gone. I don't know much about wine, but like everything else, I can learn. With all the problems I have with my family, why wouldn't I want to live here? My friends are why. Jeanne and Debbie have been with me since grammar school. I know Jeanne would come at least once a year, but I'd probably never see Debbie. Her one trip with Jeanne and me was enough for her. My friends are my family, and I need them more than ever.

We arrive back on our vineyard late one night, and I tell Angela to grab a bunch of grapes through the wire fence for us. We look around as if we are going to steal the Hope Diamond and see no one. I shine the headlights on her; it's so dark we cannot see our hands in front of us otherwise. Just as she is grabbing a handful, I blow the horn. She screams, and the only thing we see are her long arms flailing above her head. Jeanne and I laugh hysterically. For a few moments, we could be kids again.

One afternoon we spend driving off the beaten track to a village called Civita di Bagnoregio founded by the Etruscans 2500 years ago and once a thriving medieval commercial and religious center and proud birthplace of St. Bonaventure. Civita, known for its striking position atop a steep canyon overlooking the Tiber River Valley, cause many to refer to it as the Jewel on the Hill. What makes this so unique is that the only way in or out is by a mile long, steep footbridge, the old donkey path, also called "Devil's Bridge," the only link between itself and the rest of Italy. No automobiles are allowed, and supplies are ferried in on mopeds. As you make your way up, the relatively narrow bridge gets steeper as you ascend. It is said that the village is in constant danger of destruction, as the edges of the plateau collapse from erosion, leaving the buildings to crumble as their underlying support falls away. Civita became known in Italian as *il paese che muore*, "the town that is dying." It owes much of its unaltered condition to its relative isolation; the town was able to withstand most intrusions as well as the destruction brought by two world wars. Only recently has Civita been experiencing a tourist revival. The population today varies from 12 to 15 people (I'm told all elderly women who have nowhere else to go or no reason to leave) in winter and swells to more than 100 in summer. It is now considered one of the 100 most endangered sites in the world due to threats it faces from erosion and unregulated tourism.

A walk through town is like walking back in time. As you make it to the top of the footbridge, you enter under its ancient stone archway, the village's only entrance. Passing through and up to Civita's only piazza, you can see one more layer of homes to both our right and left. All these homes sit on the cliffs. The views are breathtaking from any side. Lush flowers and gardens adorn nearly every home here, wherever it sits on top of this mountain. It seems surreal, the whole experience, being literally "unattached" to the rest of the world and yet still have the Internet. The town still uses the same olive press, too, estimated to be about 1,500 years old. There's only two places to eat, and one of the restaurateurs also owns the only hotel, Antico Forno B&B, a 15th century palazzo. The owner, Franco Sala, also the cook, is an American who fell in love with a woman from here. When we arrive for dinner, we, like everyone else, are seated on the terrace under the stars and lit canopies covered with grape vines, and we're fed whatever Franco made today. Wine is always included. An unforgettable night, to say the least.

At a leisurely pace, we venture from our apartment at Casa Frassi to Montalcino, world famous for its Brunello di Montalcino wine. As you approach the small, mountaintop town, the vineyards encircle it for miles and miles over the rolling hills. The sun blesses the vines all afternoon, and in this month of October, what is left of the deep purple Sangiovese grapes hang heavy. The land is kept immaculate, showing greater pride in their exquisite and very expensive wine supplied by about 120 wineries in the immediate area. We stop and go through the small town rather quickly and get back in our car to head home. Unbeknownst to us, we take a wrong turn. Suddenly we are situated on the side of a steep mountain that barely fits our car absent any side railings. We see no end in sight, and there's no way we can turn around or back up. Our only thought is safely getting off this road, and we are not concerned with the specifics of how we are going to get down this mountainside. This road was probably made for carts many hundreds of years ago, but certainly not for automobiles. No one is around, and we make the decision to just go forward. Angela is sitting in the backseat, and although she is not a heavy weight, we tell her to move to the other side of the car in an attempt to keep the weight shifted in fear of the car falling right off the cliff, and Jeanne, too, shifts her weight. How did none of us notice that we were heading off the side of a mountain? No one is blaming each other, but the tension is so thick you can cut it with a knife. I'm praying and reminding the Lord that my dad needs me back home and to please spare our lives. We inch our way forward and aren't certain if the noise we hear from the unpaved road is the noise of rocks falling below. Are we inching our way to our deaths? The only way out of the car now would be to break through the back window and crawl out. How do I explain this to the car rental company? "Your vehicle was left in Montalcino, but you'll need a helicopter to get to it. Oh, and you'll need to enter through the broken back window." "No problem, Ms. Mancuso. We appreciate your business."

We ride along the cliff for what feels like hours. Eventually, we get to level ground unscathed. I don't know how, but we do.

We say our farewells to Tuscany and head south to Positano on the Amalfi Coast. Angela makes plans to meet a cousin she found online. Since her grandparents migrated to the United States, no one has ever returned; she'd be the first. We find our way to the spot her cousin designates for us to meet. From there, he'll park his car, and we'll all go off together in our automobile. We don't know what he has in mind for the day except for meeting more relatives. By his license plate, we are able to easily find him. After their kisses and hugs, we pack into our car with her cousin riding shotgun and Angela and Jeanne in the backseat. Something begins to smell, and I'm afraid there's a problem with the car. The smell is getting worse, actually unbearable, and now I realize it's not a car smell. In my mirror, I see Angela smelling her armpits. The three of us take showers every day, so, by process of elimination, it has to be her cousin. The four of us are compacted into the car, and the only option is to role the window down. I try holding my breath, but I know that cannot be sustained. I've never smelled body odor this bad. I didn't think it was possible. He's a successful architect, not a farmer, so this is surprising and disturbing. He proceeds to remove his heavy jacket while I'm driving, and I think I'm going to pass out; I don't know what to do with my head! I'm driving, so I have to look forward, and because no one else is insured to drive, I can't ask them to switch. And the worst part is we are on our way to eat! I'm going to throw up; the stench is so outrageous, and we're going to eat!

Fortunately, the odor disappears soon after his jacket came off; the smell was coming from his coat. We can literally breathe again. He takes us to lunch at a nice restaurant for authentic Southern Italian food, and I order the ravioli. My family is from this part of the country, and I'm always ordering this dish to see if it's made as good as my mom's, my grandmother's, and now mine. I haven't found one that comes even close anywhere. We've only made cheese ravioli; any other kind were never considered. Like at home, the restaurants offer them with various fillings. Here in the South, I assume they would be more like ours, and when they arrive, I'm surprised to be wrong. Still, no ravioli comes near ours. Unlike the store brands, we make the dough without eggs, and the pasta is kneaded and rolled out by hand, no machine. They are so delicate, they could never be made commercially because, unless treated individually and with extreme care, they fall apart.

The rest of the day is spent meeting more family and more eating. The excitement of cousins from across the ocean meeting for the very first time is palpable, as if it closes a chapter in their lives and begins a new one.

We head back to our hotel in Positano, a beautiful, small town perched along the Amalfi Coast and considered to be one of the most picturesque towns on the coast. The roads are once again winding and very narrow along the high cliffs with large buses transporting day visitors by the hundreds and moving as if they were tiny Fiats. Driving in, you cannot miss the lemon and orange trees that are everywhere. They even line the streets in front of the small, quaint shops. If you're passing through in a bus, you can literally pick the low-lying fruit from your seat. The lemons are the largest I have ever seen, the size of grapefruits. Everything is lemons here: the perfumes, soaps, the ceramic plates are decorated with them and, of course, their famous Limoncello.

The town is positioned mainly in an enclave in the hills leading down to the coast on the Tyrrhenian Sea. As such, from our bedroom window we can see nearly every hotel positioned on the sides of the mountain that encircle us. I don't know how high we are located, but there are 400 steps from our lobby to the beach, and we are not even near the top. From any point, the view is gorgeous. But we are suddenly awakened in the middle of the night by the crowing of a rooster that continues all night long! I'm no farmer, but I've only heard about roosters crowing at sunrise. Wasn't this how the farmers awakened each day? But crowing in the dark and all through the night? There are thousands of tourists in this city, and you'd have to be deaf to sleep through this. How is this allowed? With our luck, we'd find the one nocturnal rooster that would keep us up all week!

Jeanne is turning 50 this week. She's terribly saddened over the collapse of her third marriage. This one she really loved and sadly still does. Her first husband was killed just 13 months after they married in a car accident when she was merely 20, and she married Eddie, her second husband, on the rebound. Together they had three kids and stayed married for 12 years, most of them unhappily. For her birthday, she wants to spend the day visiting Ravello, a neighboring resort town on the coast, and walk through their famous gardens before taking in their shops. From the beach in Positano, we see a beautiful restaurant one flight up overlooking the water with long, white drapes that encircle the half moon shaped perimeter of the terrace. It's so striking I feel I'm looking at a movie. It's perfect for this special occasion.

After dinner, Angela and I want to surprise Jeanne with a cake. And who better to sing Happy Birthday than our gorgeous waiter? Angela excuses herself and says she's going to the bathroom, but she's really going to ask the waiter about a cake. He speaks English, but it's apparently limited because when Angela waves him in her direction, he thinks she's asking him to assist her in the BATHROOM! His face drops in disbelief. I don't know if he ever thought it was funny, but we certainly did.

As we spend our last night walking along this magnificent beach, my phone rings. My stomach is unnerved with the potential news that could be on the other end. It can be from anyone of our families about anything! It's Angela's youngest son calling to say good-bye to his mom as he enters the military the following morning. It is post 9/11, and the uncertainty of everything weighs on all of us. Here we are in this stunning setting, the three of us with heavy hearts, and our lives are moving toward dramatic changes. We're all scared, and rightfully so.

We are Rome bound. How I love this city. It's as if I lived there in another life. I'm not even a city girl, but Rome steals my heart, always has from the very first time I saw the Coliseum in 1970. I couldn't believe my eyes, like a four year old visiting Disney World for the first time. And that is where this love affair I have with Italy started. Knowing its history, the Coliseum takes my breath away every time I return. How lucky I am to have experienced living just two blocks away from it the summer of my junior year in high school. And like my first kiss, the Coliseum would always have the memory of my first Gelato.

Of the three of us, I'm the only one that is religious. Ever since Grandma's spirit started to show up nine years ago, I've rarely missed a Sunday Mass. I tell Jeanne and Angela that I am taking them to Mass at the Vatican the following morning, and I'm very surprised when they don't give me a problem about it. I make the assumption Mass starts at noon and aim to get there by 11. We walk over the Ponte Sant'

Angelo, a beautiful pedestrian bridge crossing the Tiber, and make our way up to Piazza San Pietro, Saint Peter's Square, just a few minutes away. The street is nearly as wide as the piazza itself, and people are everywhere. The line to get into the Vatican is blocks long, and each person is being checked before entering. The line moves quickly, and we are finally able to enter. But once inside, it is standing room only in the back of the church, and we are shoulder to shoulder with other churchgoers. Mass has started, and I can see the priest celebrant from this long distance. The first thing that strikes me is his enormous hat. It's too large! I turn to the man next to me, and he confirms my belief: It's Pope John Paul II giving the Mass! How did I get this lucky? Now I'm angry at myself for not arriving earlier. Had we been on time, we'd be able to get a seat and be closer to the Pope. I'll never get this opportunity again!

For his safety, he'll never walk down the aisle to the back where I can see him up close. They'd never allow that. I'm standing next to the center aisle, but I move after receiving communion so that others could receive easily. What a mistake that becomes because I was very wrong about the Pope not coming down the aisle. As he's approaching, I could see his mitre, the ceremonial headdress, but I'm too short to see over the people in front of me. Had I stayed where I was, he would have been just a couple of feet away from me as he passed. But Angela has moved, and now she is next to the aisle, and she has a camera. At least I'll have that..................... Not. Angela would lose one role of film from this trip, and it's this one!

The day has come to return home. I miss my dad terribly. I really like the woman the county sent to stay with him, and even though I have phoned home once a week, I want to see him with my own eyes. I want to hug him and feel his arms around me. No one has ever loved me more.

Our taxi leaves us at the curb, and we wheel our own luggage into the terminal. But we can't find our flight on the board. While I remain with the luggage, the other two search the terminal. When they have no luck, I try. It's getting closer to departure, and we can't find our counter. After some time, I realize we were in the domestic terminal and not international - and we are going to miss our flight.

Jeanne needs to return today because she has no one to help with her animals, Angela has to return to work or run the risk of losing her new job, and I don't have anyone scheduled for Ray beyond today. Angela runs to the counter first, and all seats are taken. After some time, one seat becomes available, and she takes it. Jeanne hasn't arrived back yet and doesn't know the situation. I go to the counter next, and I'm told they have no seats. After a while, a first-class ticket becomes available when the passenger was a no-show and gives me the seat. By the time Jeanne arrives back and finds out she is probably going to have to wait until the later flight that afternoon and return home alone, she's very upset at the thought of being separated. I don't want to leave her, but I'm stuck, too. Fortunately, a seat becomes available for her at the last moment, but she has to fly with Angela in coach. Considering I was the driver the entire vacation, I don't feel bad for one second. But they do!

***

Arriving home, I was elated to see my father, and, he, me. He rarely walked anymore, but he would stand if I was holding onto him. So, on the night of my arrival home, I asked him to slow dance with me, something he loved to do. The idea was to give him a little exercise I thought would benefit him. But the dancing was too much for him, and we ended up in the emergency room that night. Fortunately, it was only a matter of his blood sugar levels dropping, and we happily came home the following morning. He was 87 years old and still looked terrific regardless. Not a wrinkle on his face, and he still had most of his hair that was more pepper than salt. When he'd smile at me, my heart smiled back. I was always proud to be his daughter.

The woman the agency provided was great with Dad. She was originally from Africa and had a thick accent that made it difficult to understand her most of the time. But she was always laughing, and that created happiness around her. She could talk endlessly, and I was always curious to know how much, if any, of these stories I hear can I actually believe. I never knew. I only needed to feel that Ray was safe, and given the alternative of putting him in a nursing home while I was away, I knew I made the best choice - for both of us. Dad was well kept while I was away, especially with Rose, Aunt Katie, and Joe stopping by frequently to check in. Cousin Cathy slept at our home with little Samantha to oversee things at night. She refused to take money for her help, so I paid her in Italian gifts: an 18 carat gold necklace from the Ponte Vecchio and other Italian finds I picked up along the way, and Samantha received a gorgeous black leather jacket from Siena. Everyone was happy. A Win/Win.

My sister visited one more time since I arrived home, and we wouldn't see her again for some time afterwards. No contact whatsoever. I asked if someone in her household could help me transport Dad from his wheelchair to the bed, but I was denied. I was told "it was too much to ask." It was easier to hate me than to help Dad. Aside from this occurrence, none of us have spoken to each other in five years. I haven't spoken to Mom's sister, Aunt Dee, in four. I greatly miss having a family. If only they would have helped a little, I'd be happy. But I was refused every time.

Angela became so engrossed in her life with her new boyfriend, she never bothered to keep in touch with her new found family in Italy. They were so happy to see her, and, she, them, that I never expected their relationship to end so abruptly and so quickly!

Jeanne returned to the chaos of her horrific divorce and got relatively little help from any of her lawyers.

I needed to forget Preston and the drama, but with Richard visiting us often, that became impossible. I brought the pain on myself, and I rued the day we met. I had only myself to blame.

My only wish is for Dad to stay well enough for me to return to Italy next year when I'm 50. I need to hold onto hope!

Chapter Six

A UTERUS WOULD BE JUST ONE MORE THING TO HURT

Life at Home: 2003

I am turning 50 this year, and the only gift I want is to go back to Italy. A 50th birthday present to myself. Dad is diminishing, but I believe he's well enough for me to take two weeks as long as I have him covered with good caregivers 24/7. I continue to have no relationship with my siblings or Mom's sister, Aunt Dee, whom I miss the most. My only escape is the English horseback riding lessons I recently started, and I'm even more excited to be learning on retired thoroughbreds and Arabians. It's the only time I feel alive. My goal is to learn to jump.

I stopped working completely late last year when Angela tells me she overheard one of Dad's helpers yell and threaten to hit him. He was growing more confused and more difficult to handle, and she just didn't have the capacity to deal with him any longer. This means he is with me 24/7, and the only help I'm receiving is a few hours a week from the Veterans' Administration.   I wrote the VA and pleated for more help, stating, "It would be cheaper for you to keep him at home with me instead of putting him into one of your facilities."   I wrote how Dad had been the proudest veteran I had ever met and how he spoke every day of his time in the service during WWII with only the highest regard, how decades later he continued to repeat the same stories over and over, and how Mom would yell: "Ray, Ray, it's like you left the Army yesterday!" and we'd all laugh.   They apparently felt my pain and desperation because they responded the very same day, providing me someone Monday-Friday for two hours.   This would be the second time the Veterans

Administration came through for this solider, and they would come through quickly! Someone else actually cared, and it turned out to be the VA!

Dad is not as alert, and I think the meds are to blame, so I make certain that his meals are always something he particularly likes. His kidneys are not working as well, and, for that reason, I rarely give him protein anymore with the exception of my homemade ravioli, his favorite food as well. Actually, they are the favorite food to just about everyone in our family: aunts, uncles, cousins; everyone. They've only been made on the holidays or a birthday request from me. Making them was a big thing for as long as I can remember. My mom was so good at making them quickly and taught me the same. Grandma and Mom were the only ones who knew how to make them, and when Mom became sick and it was apparent she wasn't going to live many more holidays, I had her teach me. It's not Christmas or Easter, but every day Dad's with me, it's a holiday. No matter how tired he is, when he's wheeled to the kitchen table and sees those ravioli, life miraculously springs back into him. Suddenly, there's a will to live. And he always says the exact same thing: "Oh......., I like these!"

Richard continues to visit, but we no longer work together. He's enormously irritating, and half the time I fight with him over an insulting remark he makes. He'll say anything in an attempt to impress me. He is too drunk and too stoned to accept there's not a chance in hell; never was. But he still helps with Ray. Merely someone assisting my father in the bathroom while I'm cooking is a great help. I appreciate any minute someone gives. I reciprocate by inviting him to dinner several nights a week and always include Dad's famous antipasto, our other specialty. Richard loves to gossip, especially about Preston, who he still doesn't know the extent of the relationship I actually had with him. He'd be terribly jealous, and it's none of his business anyway. I don't want to hear about Preston, but the stories are crazy enough that anyone would repeat them. I desperately want to forget Preston, and he's making it impossible. Preston's second marriage wasn't working out, and he was having great difficulties financially due to lawsuits with both his first wife and a former employer. He had already spent hundreds of thousands of dollars fighting his former boss over a contract dispute when Preston hired Richard, and the only ones getting ahead were the attorneys. His lawyer tells him to file personal bankruptcy, and as a result, things started to implode. He needed cash to settle with his first wife, but due to the bankruptcy, he couldn't get a loan, not from the banks and not from his friends who had left him when he remarried. Not one of them wanted to be in her company. He goes for a loan to the people he thought were his only salvation: The Boys! But The Boys scam him, and things turned from really bad to worse. He became acutely aware that they were not going to go away when they started to follow his daughter and grandchildren! They telephoned saying, "Wouldn't it be a shame if anything happened to your kids." That's when he buckled to their demands. His next home would be the Big House.

When my friends and I were in Italy last year, we saw a group of people on horseback riding through Montalcino and thought it was the coolest thing I had ever seen - Italy on horseback! Several of my cousins had horses, and occasionally I would get a chance to ride with them. Dad wouldn't consider buying me one no matter how much I begged, and the love of riding never waned, albeit so infrequent.

After we returned home from our Italian vacation last year, Jeanne heard of a horseback riding tour through Tuscany, and I immediately called to inquire. I have seen nearly every movie made in Italy, so when I'm told they ride into Brolio where the movie *"Stealing Beauty"* was filmed, I knew this was the tour for me. There are only two tours like this during the year, and I'd select the one during harvest when it's cooler and the vines are in full bloom.

I'm told that the trip requires that I at least know how to canter, a gait faster than a trot but not as fast as a gallop, and much, much smoother than a trot. I have several months before I leave, so I'll double up on the lessons to bring me up to the minimum level required. I send my large non-refundable deposit, and I'll be fine by the time the tour begins .... So Not!

Shortly after mailing my deposit, I receive a call from my gynecologist telling me there are pre-cancerous cells present, and I need a hysterectomy. Just like that; like he's telling me I need an oil change. "Ok," I tell him; "as soon as I return in October." "No, it must be done now," he replies. Now! Are you kidding me? And he's talking about a full hysterectomy, to boot. I'm leaving in three months, I've never cantered, I cannot get my deposit back, and THIS is the year I'm turning 50; only this year!

I schedule help for Dad in our home for the time I'm hospitalized. I'm petrified of the pain since my last surgery merely five months after Dad moved in. The pain literally took my breath away. The doctor assures me he'll help me with the pain, and because my friend Debbie knows him personally, he agrees she'll be available to me when I reach the recovery room. Knowing Debbie will be there means everything; I feel safe.

Four painful days are spent in the hospital, and when I'm discharged and Debbie picks me up, I cry because I am afraid to go home with the amount of help Dad requires now, and I don't know how I'll be able to handle him after major surgery. He needs to be lifted in and out of bed and into his wheelchair, and if he is tired, he becomes more confused and frightened. I am very happy I was able to book the same woman we had last year. She was always happy and genuinely seemed to care about him. But it is different this time; she has fallen in love. It would be such a great love story except for the fact that he's a married minister. They are from the same village in Africa and had one chance meeting as children. They never forgot each other, and decades later they would find each other through an organization in the United States of people from their hometown. I don't think they ever had the opportunity of meeting each other more than once since they've found each other due to their lives and lack of transportation, but they are constantly on the phone with each other. I'd hear her phone ring all through the night across the hall from my bedroom, and I could hear her laughing and giggling. I am happy she is happy, but I can't see how this is going to end well.

Dad doesn't walk any more, and it is often difficult getting him out of bed or up from the couch. Some nights I end up calling the police for help getting him off the floor when he's fallen. They are always so gracious about it. He's more disoriented, and he can say very few words now. I'm told to not lift anything or run the risk of ripping my staples out. But, by the very next morning, the aide can't get him out of bed, and Dad is hitting her when she attempts to get him out of bed. He's too tired to get up, but I am concerned about him eating breakfast and taking his insulin. I need to intercede because I'm the only one he trusts, the only one who is not frightening him, and I take the chance and lift him into his wheelchair. As he's placed into his chair, his head hanging low, he lifts it, pointing his finger at me, and says, "I did it for YOU!" Back down his head goes until he's wheeled into the kitchen and sees his beautiful breakfast.

I'm able to climb stairs within five days of my surgery, and as a result of the exercise I am getting with Ray, my recovery is minimal and nearly pain free. God must have sent an angel because I never had a problem lifting him, not that day or any other day to come.

When the equestrian representative calls to confirm details, I tell her about the surgery and inform her that I was not able to take any more riding lessons. There's complete silence on the other end. At least I told her. Unless there's an issue with Ray, I'm going forward with this trip.

After eight and a half years of volunteering for the homeless, I resign from the board. I had been blind. I grew up in a respectable neighborhood, and that's all I knew of people. This, however, was another world. The reports from the director of what was happening with the guests really disheartened me. My soul was in this mission, but they abused us, our generosity. Over 90 percent of the people we helped over the years were not the kind of people we were established to help. Instead, these are people who don't want to help themselves. They don't want to work! Seven and a half of these years spent volunteering were while my own father was ill, and I was already beyond inundated. I wonder when I became a fool! I'm embarrassed it took me this long to come to this realization. I find it hard to accept how the government's money is so wrongly distributed, but it's staring me in the face. How is this allowed to happen?

I specifically request the same woman from the agency to stay with Dad during my vacation. I'm assured it's not a problem.

But two days before I leave, I call to confirm the time, and I'm informed they don't even have us down as clients that week! They don't care about our previous conversations, and I have to settle for a stranger the day before my departure. It's too late to do anything about it, and I once again reassure myself it's okay to leave given Cousin Cathy and Samantha are sleeping at the house and Cousin Sammy is on the second floor. But my gut isn't comfortable with the woman! If necessary, I'll fly home early.

When I leave home, I tell Dad's aide to call my sister and inform her I'm out of the country in the event she wants to visit her father. She hasn't seen him in over a year.

***

I land in Rome and make the three-and-a-half hour drive north to Casa Frassi in Castellina where I'll spend one night before heading to the riding center. I'm over the moon happy when I pull into their long, cypress lined driveway all the way up to the main house. My room for tonight is on the second floor of the main building. The shutters open to a stunning view everywhere I look. To my right, I can see the vineyards, and to my left is an olive grove.

After a typical Tuscan buffet breakfast of hard bread, cheeses, cakes, cereals with too much chocolate, and Tuscan meats (not my favorite meal) on their beautiful terrace, I head northeast to a small Tuscan village for my horseback riding tour. The owner, Jenny, is originally from England, so there's no communication problems. She helps me to the second floor with my oversized luggage, commenting I had to be American with this much baggage. She shows me to my small room with a single bed against the wall, but it has a great view and an adequate en suite bathroom. This is a riding vacation, not a luxury spa. After placing my luggage in the room where it barely fits, we go to the common living room just feet away. There's a very large stone fireplace that already has a fire going and a wall full of books. Books are in every room. Jenny pours me a glass of wine and tells me all about herself: she moved to Italy decades earlier to work at the university and has never left. She became very good friends with Pietro, the man who worked the land next door. He knew everything about the land and how to grow all kinds of fruits and vegetables, how to prune olive trees and establish a vineyard, and he could cook! He was born here and lived through the most difficult times. He was a true peasant farmer. When Jenny decided she wanted to build her dream of owning and running a riding centre, she took Pietro and his entire family with her. By now, Jenny was a single mom with a son, and the two families merged, in a sense.   Jenny purchased property that had several stone structures and eventually converted one into a home for Pietro and his family.   In the Tuscan countryside, they only allow building on existing foundations to keep the stunning landscape protected. It is even difficult to get a permit for a swimming pool. Tuscans know what they have here, and they are not going to let the landscape change unless God Himself does it.

Pietro is up there in age, and although he speaks no English, we're able to communicate somewhat with the limited Italian I know. It is like having a beloved grandfather around that cooks great! He's led such an interesting life, Jenny has written a book about him called *Pietro's Story*. It describes his life as a peasant, how they lived, how they had no indoor plumbing until Mussolini made it law, how they ate, what they did for entertainment, and what and how they harvested each month; the true definition of the salt of the earth.

Within a few hours, the other guests I will be riding with arrive. There are only three other people besides Jenny and myself consisting of a man and a woman from Colorado and another single woman from Connecticut. Jenny typically gets quite a few more riders from the United States, but things are different this year. The change from the Lire to the Euro has made a tremendous difference overnight; the U.S. dollar was no longer stronger than Italy's currency. Thankfully, they didn't cancel the tour.

As we sit around drinking our wine in the living room and getting to know each other, I learn that the two other female riders have been riding their entire lives. They can easily jump three-foot concrete walls on horseback. The only gentleman in the group cannot ride as well as them, but he can canter, and it's not his first riding tour either. When they come to me, I don't know what to say. For the first time in my life, I am evasive because I've become worried that Jenny is

130

hesitating about me riding after hearing their stories. I tell her I've been riding over the years but not steadily and that I've been taking lessons. She asked how many, and I tell her at least 50. That's probably too high a number, but I've never counted, and it sounds like that will be acceptable.

Pietro cooks dinner, and we all sit together at one long table in the dining room. The building we are in is hundreds of years old - and it will be here for hundreds more. The tables are covered with linens, and the table settings are more than adequate for a farmhouse. Aside from the horses, there's various barn animals roaming the property and a huge, friendly, long haired dog that greets you. My room is small, and I have a very small bathroom, but once I open my shutters, the view more than makes up for the size.

From the pass-through in the kitchen to the dining room, Jenny is handed each course to be served family style. A variety of *bruschetta,* pomarola, a typical Italian sauce over spaghetti, chicken and fresh vegetables from the garden cooked with olive oil and garlic, Tuscan biscuits with almonds, fresh fruit, and homemade *tiramisu.* Wine, of course, as much as you want. From here, we head to bed. Tomorrow is our first day out riding. We have a morning ride scheduled through olive groves, vineyards, and woodlands of the Arno Valley, passing farmhouses and medieval hamlets. I can't wait, but I'm scared shitless.

The next morning I'm up and dressed in my equestrian outfit, half chaps and all, and meet up with everyone in the dining room for breakfast. When we're done, we walk about 100 feet behind the home to the stables where there are 18 immaculately groomed horses. Jenny treats them like they are her children, and it shows. The other riders are assisting with saddling up, but I don't have a clue. I explain that when I've taken lessons the horses were always saddled already. I'm <u>very</u> much out of their league.

We all mount our horses, and I'm last. Jenny knows to give me the least aggressive animal, and all I need is one that will keep up with the others. Each of us are on our respective horses, and we are handed a whip. I don't want a whip; I don't want to beat anything, but they insist in the event it's needed to move them along. I'm reminded that I'm not in a ring anymore; I'm in the country where there's animals like wild boar that can scare the horses easily. Jenny is very fussy, too, about where to hold the reins; she doesn't want you pulling on their mouths. If I pull too tight, I'm afraid they'll try to throw me, and if the reins are too loose, they can take off running. It's becoming more frightening by the moment.

It's a tremendous difference over riding western style where the only training is getting on the horse and kicking it to move faster while holding onto the horn for dear life. All I ever wanted to do was gallop from the moment I mounted my first horse. Trail riding wasn't enough for me. I'd always press the guide to let loose, but normally I'd have to steal the time by deliberately kicking the horse against their instructions. But English riding cannot be any more different. The saddle has no horn, and it's half the size of a western one. You position nearly every muscle in your body a certain way while the 1,000 plus pounds of animal between your legs has a mind of its own. Head up, shoulders back, arms out, thumbs up and pinch the rein between the thumb and index finger, back straight, legs tight and against the horse, and, of course, feet against the horse and heels down. For me, that sounds doable if the horse is plastic and I just put a quarter in the machine to get it to move.

We ride through the village and cross the main street, carefully looking to see if any cars or vespas are approaching. The horses scare easily, and we should always stay together in the group. We reach the neighboring village with acres and acres of vineyards. We're formed in a straight line, and suddenly Jenny looks back and informs us we are going to make our first canter right through the vineyards! She yells, "canter," and the horses know exactly what to do in both Italian and English; I don't even need to kick. I feel like I'm in a movie. I didn't dream this big. I take a deep breath, and all of my concentration is on my feet and keeping my heels down. If I don't and the horse stops short, I'll go flying forward over his head like Christopher Reeves. I'm both elated with the most excitement I have ever felt in my life and desperately afraid at the same time. Here I am riding with all these experienced riders, and I've never once even cantered. Of course, Jenny doesn't know that fact. On our last day, I'll come forward and tell her the truth. It will be funny then. But not today.

On our second day of riding, we go out for a much longer stretch - five hours. We ride up through the pine, oak, and chestnut woods to the top of the Chianti mountains and enjoy a magnificent view of the Chianti region and the Arno Valley. After the first 45 minutes, I'm finding it nearly impossible to post one more time, and I have hours yet to go. It's like taking a weight lifter who has never gone over 50 lbs. and asking him to lift 200 lbs. It just doesn't work that way. I've waited for this experience ever since I saw *Bonanza* the very first time, and I've never given any thought to not being able to post because I've never been in an English saddle longer than an hour.

It is apparent to Jenny I'm not nearly as experienced as she first thought, but she cannot change anything now. She shows us how she wants us to canter, leaning forward and holding onto the horse's mane while actually leaning on him, a two-point canter. I should know this, too. My first reaction is that even a horse won't like the weight against his neck and possibly try to throw me, but I'm assured otherwise. After a few canters like this, I quickly favor this "half-seat" over a trot where you constantly have to post. My legs cannot lift me up and down one more time today, nor can my ass take the constant bouncing. I'm quickly becoming more comfortable with cantering, but my heart is in my throat each and every time.

Jenny tries and shows me how to move with the horse so that my butt is not bouncing off his back and affecting him. I feel like I'm seven years old again in ballet class, and I cannot remember one step from another while attempting a pirouette and nearly pirouette out the second floor window. Mom dropped the class for me and Nicey that day. Jenny's telling me to watch his legs, feel his gait, and let my butt just "kiss" the saddle. With me trying to concentrate on every muscle in my body while this 1,000 plus pound animal is running between my legs, it would be easier for me to kiss his ass! This is harder than my hysterectomy.

In the morning, we ride out to the ancient Abbey of Coltibuono where Sergio, Pietro's son, has arrived in a van and has a hot picnic lunch with linen table cloths and wine set up for us. We dismount, tie the horses to the trees, and head for a great Italian picnic lunch. You cannot find a bad meal here. When we're able to remove ourselves from the table, we visit the Abbey's wine cellar and garden. After two glasses of wine, I put my helmet back on, mount, and suddenly I'm Dale Evans. Amazing how the wine improves my skills! By the time we return to Castellina, all I can do is slide off my horse. And I get to do this again tomorrow! God help me! Tonight's accommodations are at a beautiful palazzo in Castellina - behind the medieval walls. Wow!

Every day I'm taken back to my childhood dream of living on the Ponderosa with the Cartwrights and arrive into town on horseback. Each day we ride through another village or hamlet, I'm living my dream.

The following morning we ride southward through the heart of the Chianti Classico area with its soft hills, vineyards, and oak woodlands. We continue past the castle of San Polo-in-Rosso and picnic near a winery where Sergio will be waiting for us with a hot lunch and then ride onto a farm where the horses are trained for the famous "Palio" horse race. Tonight's accommodations are at the same beautiful palazzo.

But something has happened with the stables Jenny arranged for the horses, and she cannot change the itinerary now. It's not as if we're driving and can just take another road; we're on horseback. So, as we wine, dine, and sleep in an incredible, ancient palazzo, Jenny is camped out with her horses. She did, however, make sure to have a large bottle of wine in the tent. I never thought to ask if she took a gun.

The following day we meet for another great lunch on the side of a farmhouse, a seemingly vacant home. When we leave any property, there's never a trace of us except for horse manure. And the farmers welcome it for their crops. That's why Jenny freely runs through her neighbors' vineyards with the horses. Many of the properties in Tuscany are vacant, but the land itself is worked for the production of wine and olive oil. We sit and eat, and while the others are still sipping wine and laughing, I take my Nikon and walk around the property to see if there are any good shots. I never go near a window; I am merely walking about 20 feet from the house. As I approach the rear of the home, I hear a man yelling loudly. I stand there for a moment, and when he sees me, he goes absolutely crazy. I don't understand what he's screaming, but I know it's not a happy voice and he's coming straight for me! Jenny and Sergio hear him and immediately come to my aid, and I walk away in total fear. Jenny and Sergio take his verbal abuse for some time before he walks away to return to the man he was screaming at. Fortunately, we had already eaten and were already packing up. I can't imagine what would have happened had the man saw us all sitting there and eating while the horses were tied to his trees.

As all of us are ready to mount our horses, we hear even a bigger commotion. The other gentleman had started a fire in the house while soldering something. Sergio and his son run into the house and put out the fire. The homeowner who went crazy never even said thank you! We all wanted to know what he was screaming about, but neither Jenny or Sergio would ever say. It was too offensive to repeat. I can only assume it was something nasty about Americans. Why wouldn't they tell us otherwise?

At dinner one night, I confide in the other three riders that my biggest fear is falling off and be stepped on by a horse. One rider confides she's been riding for 50 years and has never seen that happen. Armed with this knowledge, I'm able to ride tomorrow with more confidence.

The following day we are out in the country where Jenny has ridden for years. This time, however, there is a new fence where we were to cross. We ride up further, and Jenny decides she wants to make the crossing, but the horses would have to jump a ravine. A jump! I wait patiently while the others have no trouble, and now it's my turn. I tighten my helmet and kick my horse. I'm so thrilled when I realize that I made it over the ravine, and as I pick my head up, I'm hit in the head with a branch I didn't clear. The others are moving forward ahead of me, and I'm leaning backwards while my horse is moving forward. I think I can manage to raise my body, but with him moving forward, I slowly, so very slowly, continue to lean backwards until finally falling head first on the cement pavement, maybe the only piece of cement in the entire village! It's like I'm in a movie and I'm the stuntwoman. God sent another angel because had I not tightened my

136

helmet, it probably would have fallen off, and I would have suffered a brain injury. I imagine God thinking: "I'm paying these angels overtime this week, Debbie. Get it together." Little did I know, it was far from over.

I quickly mount the horse, and the only thing hurting is my ego. I assure Jenny I'm fine and to continue as planned. We ride for another hour when my helmet slips over my eyes and blinds me. Jenny has taught me that when we're cantering through the woods to just put my head all the way down next to the horse's neck so I won't get hit in the head by a branch. Yeah, I just failed that lesson an hour ago. But this time, I'm completely blinded by the helmet, and I have my head next to the horse's neck, not one inch above, and the speed of the canter is picking up. What I cannot see is that my horse is attempting to take over the one in front of us. He's fucking racing! What I also don't see is that the other horses are stopping. The next thing I know I am on the ground - again! I fell so fast I was on the ground before I even knew I left the saddle! Fortunately, I fell onto soft dirt. My horse, having no room to move, goes to put one leg down right ON MY LEFT ARM and then immediately retracts. The people in the group tell me that when the horse felt the ground wasn't stable, he immediately picked his leg up, and that's what saved my arm from being crushed like a tomato. Didn't we just discuss this last night when I spoke of my biggest fear? Jenny was beside herself saying how no one has fallen in over a year and here I go and fall twice. I can't get upset with her; she doesn't want anything to happen to me. They are all shocked when I have the nerve to get back in the saddle after two falls, but truth is I'm so embarrassed I have to. Actually, I never even brush myself off, figuring I am going down again anyway! They loudly cheer me on and comment how strong Jersey girls are.

Unbelievably, I sleep through the night with no pain whatsoever. When I awaken, however, there's a black and blue from my elbow to my wrist - but still no pain. Thank you, Jesus; we ride again!

I stay behind the following day at Jenny's advice, and I'm told they rode like nuts through the woods. I was smart not to go. But I do make the ride the next morning to the magnificent 12th century Castle of Brolio where Chianti wine was invented in the 19th century and where they filmed *Stealing Beauty* on their grounds. We ride past the house, back down the dirt road to the narrow in-ground pool used in the movie that's surrounded by oversized Bamboo stalks, and then continue to the enormous, majestic tree that is an important backdrop in the movie.

I mail postcards to all my doctors telling them about my falls and I now have the title of Village Idiot here. No one could believe I would be riding like this just three months after major surgery, but I proved them wrong. I end the postcard saying: "I'm glad I don't have my uterus anymore. It would be just one more thing to hurt."

The end of the week has come, and I'm grateful I wasn't killed or disabled. I have one more week at an apartment in the Crete Senesi region of Tuscany. We say our good-byes, and by now Jenny knows my full situation about the surgery and how the touring company just didn't want to lose my business even though I wasn't qualified. I don't think she blames me at all. As it turns out, this is the most difficult riding course they give the entire year. It's also the nicest time to ride between the perfect weather and vineyards in full bloom. Luckily, I was able to ride about 80 of the 100 miles over the week. It was a miracle I wasn't even hurt!

I'm driving out of Jenny's village when I hear a beep on my phone. I never realized this entire past week that I was out of range. I pull over and hear a message from home; Dad collapsed and they took him to the hospital. The caregiver the agency sent was injecting him with insulin but not making any effort to see that he ate, and his blood sugar dropped so low he passed out. If the paramedics were not called, he would have gone into a coma and died. I'm even told that the paramedics scolded her twice over the care she was giving him! They had been to the home more than once already! Unforgivable. My gut was right about her.

I drive onto the Val d'Orcia region to the agency in Montalcino which borders the Crete Senesi. All I can think about is my father while driving through one of the most scenic routes in the area, past Montepulciano, and never notice the beauty surrounding me. I keep thinking how lazy this aide is; how she allowed this to happen. I'm enraged. When she arrived the night before I left, I went food shopping and asked her what she ate. She replied, "salmon." When asked what else, she replied, "just salmon." I thought, oh, sure, that's all you ever eat. You think I'm that stupid? I purchased a few pieces and that was it. I didn't like her from the very beginning, but I wasn't expecting her disregard for his well being. When Rose would drop by, she was always watching television and paying no attention to Dad, and she was annoyed that Rose even stopped by to see him. Cousin Cathy and Rose didn't want to ruin my vacation, and no one expected his life to be in danger considering she comes through The Veterans Administration. She had to have been vetted. We were all wrong.

I finally reach Montalcino and run into the agency. My agent, Valentina, speaks English, and I explain my situation about my father. I can't calm down. With her is the manager of the home, Fabio. She introduces us, and when he realizes I don't speak Italian, he drops his head into his hands in disbelief. The way he's carrying on, you'd think I was a serial killer. The agent assures him it will be fine, and now I'm uncomfortable because he's upset. She tells me to follow him in my car; he'll take me to the home in the countryside. We drive for 15 minutes and turn onto a long dirt road. We're climbing the mountain, turning onto more dirt roads, and I don't know how I'll find the apartment again once I leave it. And I also don't know if my vacation will come to a sudden end and I'll have to return home to take care of Dad. I'll do whatever he needs.

I'm in San Giovanni d'Asso, the oldest hamlet in the entire Crete Senesi region and known for its famous black, very costly truffles. We reach the top of the mountain, and there's an electric gate. My door is on the second floor with stone steps outside leading to it, just like at Maria's pig farm. Fabio takes my luggage and drags it upstairs. He, too, makes a comment about the size of the luggage, albeit in Italian. This I understand. The home has two separate units, but I'm the only tenant this week. That frightens me. I don't know if I'm even going to be able to find my way back once I leave the top of this mountain, and if and when I do, I'll be alone in this very dark place. There's a motorized gate, but if someone wants to get in, I imagine they can easily jump the fence.

I can tell Fabio likes me and has invited me to join him for lunch. But I'm so upset and worried about my father, I decline. He actually understands me. A short time passes and my phone rings; I see it's from home. My heart drops, and I'm terrified to answer. Happily, I'm told that my father was released from the hospital and sent home that day. What a relief, and I don't have to fly back prematurely now. Fabio breaks out the wine.

I food shop at the Coop in Torrenieri which closes for siesta at 1 and reopens at 4. My biggest adjustment in Italy is getting used to the country's schedule: up early, shop, lunch, siesta, shop, late dinner, walk. And the best restaurants in the small villages fill up quickly for lunch, so if you arrive after they're full, you don't get a table that day. The small villages are dead quiet during siesta, and many of their cafes are closed as well.

Fabio stops by often during the week, and one day he invites me to visit an ancient monastery with him, the Abbey of Monte Oliveto Maggiore. I have an Italian dictionary on my lap, but it's quickly becoming boring learning about each other "one word at a time." He is not a romantic interest to me, but maybe he would be if he was single. But he's not. I do like having a friend in Italy other than Maria and Angelo in case I need another one, but I know he's hoping for more. Don't they all! At least most of the other Italians I have befriended over the years have known a little English. I like his flirting, and I could see how an afternoon among the vineyards and sipping wine could change things between friends, but as sweet as he is, I am not sleeping with him.

During the afternoons, I visit a nearby village like San Quirico d'Orcia, Castiglione d'Orcia, Asciano, the medieval city of Montepulciano, or back to Montalcino where I'd get a parking ticket for 33.60 Euros. I really need to learn how to read the signs better! I drive for hours in each direction up and down the rolling hills just checking out the Senese terrain. It's not like the Chianti region where it's all vineyards of Sangiovese grapes and olive trees outside of the historic centers, but the rolling hills around me are full of grain and the remains of the sunflowers, and the vines around Montalcino are full of the Brunello grapes, a mere 15 minutes away from me. From my apartment, I can see Montalcino lit up at night, perched high on the hill. It's gorgeous. I window shop mostly and always stop for at least a cappuccino or a gelato. I sleep in, my other favorite pastime, and I'm always aware of the time because every night I race the sun home as it sets over the mountain. If I'm not home by dark, I may never find my way back. The car rental company doesn't insure you if you go off a paved road, and I am definitely far off a paved road.

My last day in Tuscany arrives, and Fabio is very sorry to see me go. We both expect I'll return here. I've made the decision that when Dad does leave, I'll return to Italy immediately. I'm hoping to live and work at Altesino and ride the Arabians. It's the only thing I can comprehend doing without Dad. From Italy, I'll make my decisions.

We say our good-byes, kisses on both checks, and exit the motorized gate. Onto Rome I drive for a couple of nights before heading home. I've made reservations in the historic center at the place Jeanne found last year through her timeshare, Planet 29. But it's too close to the main train terminal for my taste. Could I afford more, I'd be nearer to the Pantheon. I'm here to shop for shoes, boots, leather bags and scarves for my friends and me, and I can still do this by foot from this location. Italy is years ahead of the United States in fashion, and it will take that long for my friends to get used to my new Italian footwear. And I'm particularly happy with the purchase of a beautiful black and white stripe Borghese dress shirt for Dad. What I really want to purchase is a beautiful Cashmere coat for Dad from here, but my heart is heavy knowing he'll never have a need for one again.

A few days later, and I'm headed home. Can't wait to hug my father! Can't wait to see his smile; that beautiful, perfect smile.

***

When I arrived home, Dad was elated to see me, and I, him. But he was unkempt. His hair was dirty, and he had body odor. He wasn't showered every day as instructed. The caregiver was scheduled to stay one more night, but she asked if she could be discharged right away. I agreed and was happy she'd be out of our lives. She advised me her son had already picked up her belongings, the little she had, and that made me suspicious. I discover later that she had helped herself to my personal belongings and how she was really treating my father, the blatant disregard for his health. I complained to the commission that oversees adult healthcare, but they could only tell me they'd watch the agency closely for other violations. Cousin Cathy was afraid to tell me everything in fear I'd cut my trip short. No one knew what to say when I phoned home. Having Cathy and Samantha there during the night probably saved his life. I was happy to give Cathy an 18-carat gold bracelet from Rome, among many other finds I'd come across along the trip, for all her efforts. She truly cared about my father, and she wasn't even a blood relation.

My sister visited Dad with her family a few times during my stay in Italy. There would be only one more visit from her, and she would have to be removed by the police! My poor, deceased mother!

Fabio, a professional photographer, and I emailed each other once I returned home, and he sent me gorgeous photographs he'd taken of the property just that day with fresh, fluffy snow covering the delicate tree blossoms. I continued to crave for Tuscany.

I still thought about Preston.............

Chapter Seven

Life at Home: 2004

It's a cold winter's day in February when Dad aspirates into his lungs, just five days before turning 89. In the hospital, the doctors send as many people to me as they do Dad, and it's then I realize just how serious it is this time. They say he has a 50 percent chance of pulling through, and I think he'll show them just how tough he really is and walk out of here in a week. They assure me he isn't in any pain; the only comfort I have. I hop onto his hospital bed, fixing his blanket, and tell him I love him. He opens his eyes, pointing his finger back and forth toward me, and repeats, "I love YOU!" He hadn't spoken in hours, and even with the ordeal of coming to the hospital, he pushes himself hard enough to get those words out. I can't breathe!

On the third day, one of his lungs collapses while I'm holding him in my arms. I scream for a nurse, and when she arrives, she can only say, "Honey, he is leaving now." But he doesn't, and the priest administers his last rites. I begin to accept he will not pull through this incident, but I can't bring myself to say good-bye. I lay next to him and say the words I never thought I could: "Dad, I know you are staying here because you don't want to leave me, but I want you to know that if you must go, I'll be ok. I don't know how, but I'll be ok. I don't want you to leave, I never want you to leave me, but I know you want to be with Mommy and Grandma. Don't worry about me anymore, Dad." My body is trembling; no tears can roll down my cheek; my face is frozen. I have given

144

him permission to leave me .... forever, the hardest thing I've ever had to do in my life! I don't mean what I said; I really can't imagine how I'll ever be ok, but I have to let him go in peace.

I wait as he lay there so quietly, never moving a muscle. Then it dawns on me, and I run to the nurse announcing: "My dad's not leaving today; he will pass on Friday when his mother from heaven will be here to pick him up." The nurse backs off, as if she saw a ghost, and then catches her composure. By now, the staff know me; I have never left his side. I shower, dress, eat and sleep here.

The nurse asks if I want to take him home to pass, and I quickly accept when I'm assured he'll have no pain. They arrange for the ambulance to transport him back home to pass in his own bed, something Mom wanted and never got. I'm getting a "final" wish; I'm getting to take Ray home!

The staff knows my personal situation and are very sympathetic to my impending loss. They send a psychologist to counsel me, but there's nothing she can say to make me feel better. Nothing! But she does give me one piece of advice I will never forget: "In the coming year, do not make any big decisions. In the next three months, the only thing you need to do each day is get up and put one foot in front of the other; that's it." I know she's right. I made the decision a year ago to return to Italy after he passed. It will be the only thing I can do for myself. I refuse to cry at home and suffer after devoting my life to making sure he had a happy one! I'll put one foot in front of the other starting in Italy.

Debbie runs to the hospital when she's notified where we are and takes it upon herself to notify my two sisters. Only one sister comes to the hospital, and Debbie serves as the family mediator. The other one tells Debbie that, "she didn't know he was even still alive!" A blatant lie.

The nurse can only arrange for his transportation home on Friday, Dad's 89th birthday, and have hospice there as well. I pack his belongings and cry when I say my good-byes to the staff.   They even ask me to call when he expires.   The ambulance carries him home on this blistery winter's morning and places him gently on his hospital bed in the bedroom that was once mine all those years ago. The home has not changed much since we moved into it new in 1964, but life could not be more different for us now. But home was home; I had worked like a dog to keep it, and I have no intentions of selling it to anyone other than myself. I just need a way to purchase it. No simple task considering I don't even have a job.

On Friday morning, Dad passes on his 89th birthday just as I predicted. Both sisters were informed of his imminent passing; one chooses to keep her hair appointment instead, and the other one never returns Debbie's second phone call.

Dad goes out peacefully, his breathing becoming shallower with each passing breathe, and he takes his final breath just an hour after returning home.   Rose, who has become a second mother to me, is with us, and Frank Sinatra is singing *Stardust* in the room.   Dad would certainly like that. My mind races to past Sunday mornings as a kid and being awakened by Frank singing *That's Life* and the smell of Mom's gravy cooking. My heart is breaking; I'm acutely aware that I am all alone now.

As difficult as it is, part of me is elated knowing his mother came for him. Even I could never have expected that. It was God's way of blessing me with the grace of letting him go. They say when a solider is fatally wounded in combat, they cry out for their mother. He was a soldier, not wounded in battle, but momma was his dying wish. And he got it!   I can't imagine the happiness, the joy, the excitement he feels seeing her today! Mamma finally arrived to take him home.

He's been waiting eight years! Drifting off to sleep, I wonder if Mom is making him ravioli. I bet Grandma bought him a car!

The youngest sister never attends the wake, the funeral, and never sends a flower or card. I cry to Uncle Leo, Dad's brother, "Won't people think he did something awful to her." Nothing could be further from the truth. Uncle Leo assures me that everyone knew the kind, gentle man he was and it would never enter their minds. She had no interest in her own father; it was only his money she wanted!

I make certain Dad goes out in style. All he really cared about was being buried with Mom. He's laid to rest in a black, double breasted Armani suit and his Borghese shirt from Rome, and I buy him a coffin befitting a saint, adorned with the Pieta' and The Last Supper. This is what he'd love; it's what he would have bought for his mom. Before he goes, though, I slip a $5 bill, a few Euros, and some Lire in his pocket in the event he runs into some of his friends at the pearly gates. He'll have enough to buy them coffee.

Rose comforts me, and I couldn't have a better person to be with me when Dad expired. She's also spiritual; she actually sees spirits. As Dad was passing over, she kept seeing two spirits walking through the house from his room to the kitchen, back and forth. She didn't tell me until after the funeral director arrived and took Dad away. She asks why on such a cold morning I opened his bedroom window. "To let fresh air in," I reply. "Something told me to do it." Rose reminds me the spirits enter through the windows to take their loved ones. When she describes the two spirits, I know they're my mother and his mother. They came together to take Dad home.

The moment Dad's attorney, Jeff, tells me it is ok to leave the country, I schedule my departure. I can't leave soon enough. At least in Italy I'll be in a different setting and won't think about the constant feuding with my family. Jeff will intervene. Although Jeff and I know each other many years and I've come to respect him while working together on the homeless mission, I know he sticks to the letter of the law. As our organization's president, every penny was accounted for. This means our friendship doesn't come between my sisters and me. It also means everything I submit needs to be documented. Over the eight years, hundreds of purchases have been made on my credit; Dad never had his own credit cards. When his cash ran out, I even paid his real estate taxes from my savings. Every single thing needs to be documented, or I won't get the money I lent him back! I have every receipt, and it's going to take me months to backtrack. I'll take as much paperwork to Italy with me as possible and start to straighten my life out from Tuscany as best I can. I am preparing for whatever fighting it takes. Because Dad had his will done before suffering the stroke, he couldn't change it, which my sisters were so acutely aware. The assets would be divided three ways regardless of the last eight years.

I want to celebrate Dad's life and the fact we accomplished our goals: keeping him out of a nursing home and maintaining ownership of his home. Regardless of all the lawyers and all the fighting, I know, without doubt, I did the right thing. Ironically, doing the right thing by Dad meant not granting Mommy's dying wish to "stay together" and "never leave your sisters." I remember thinking, why would we leave each other? Now I know why. It's killing me Mom doesn't get her dying wish, but it was never a question where Dad was going - he was going with me! He needed a protector, and no one was going to do that better than me.

I'm enrolled in school in Siena to learn Italian just six weeks after Dad's passing. The school offers several options for boarding, and I chose the least expensive, considering the length of time I'll be away, by living with a family. This way, too, I'll get to practice with my host family what I've learned during class.

But before I leave, however, Rose would anxiously tell me she had a visit from my father in her sleep and what he said: "Tell Debbie to go to Italy and be happy," she says he insisted. He even writes down a figure and tells her how much I should give my sisters of the inheritance. He doesn't bring up the subject that I have no control over it, though.

Jeanne drives me to the airport, and it's a sad good-bye knowing when I return it will be to an empty house. I can't help but recall coming home a few years ago and flying up the stairs to Dad's open arms. He couldn't say much, but he never stopped smiling. He was as happy to see me as I was him. The aides said he'd often ask, "Where's my daughter?" Everyone knew he was asking for me. The stroke never took me from him!

I push the sadness out of my mind and think about my next great adventure: Scuola Leonardo da Vinci in my favorite Tuscan city, Siena. There's something magical about this place, and now I will actually be going to school there behind the medieval walls!

I was unable to get a non-stop flight to Rome, so I have a stopover in Paris. Once I arrive Rome, I need to board a train directly to Siena and then take a taxi to my host's home. The schedule is very tight, and without missing a heartbeat, I start school the very next morning.

149

I'm excited that I'm able to fly first class this time with all the points I've accumulated on my American Express card fixing Dad's home. As I approach the counter at Charles De Gaulle Airport, the woman says to me, "Bonjour," and I gleefully reply, "Bonjour" back. I feel like I'm Carrie Bradshaw on *Sex and the City* arriving in Paris. As I pass each and every airport personnel, we repeat the same word to each other. I'm never going to get tired of this .... Not.

An older gentleman sits down next to me as we're waiting at the gate. He is from somewhere south of Rome and is returning home to visit his mother. He tells me about his hometown and his farm, how they prune olive trees, and about his mom, a strong, old Italian woman, just like Dad's five sisters. I look at my watch and tell him that our flight should have been called already, but he insists it wasn't and assures me not to worry. But the loudspeaker is so badly muffled that it cannot be understood even if you know French. Again, I tell him we should be concerned, but he continues to insist it's just a delay. I don't want to insult him - until I notice that the gate adjacent to us is going to Rome. I tell him two planes immediately next to each other wouldn't be going to the same place. With that, we both jump up and run to the gate when we're told they closed the doors and we'd have to wait eight more hours! All because I didn't want to insult a stranger! I also lose first class status for the remainder of the trip. After sitting there eight hours tied to my carry-on bags, I'm ready to slap the next person that says *Bonjour* to me!

***

I finally reach Rome but miss the last train to Siena. I'm forced to take a train to a different location and board a long, slow bus before taking a taxi to my host's home. It is midnight before I reach my destination, and class begins tomorrow morning at 8:30! Not how I had planned this at all!

The home is an apartment, and not a single family dwelling like I had hoped, and it's located four blocks outside the medieval walls, and not inside as I had requested. Those accommodations were all taken. My room is the size of a long, narrow bathroom. The single bed is against the wall, and the desk in the room sits immediately next to the door. The old, wooden desk chair where I'll study and do homework is without even a pad to sit on. The family is nice enough, but I'm not invited to use any other rooms except the bathroom and the kitchen when I eat with them. That's the arrangement they have with the school. The mom is a great cook, and that is the nicest part of being in their home.

I don't know what to expect in school. I'm 50 years old, and I wonder if I'll be the oldest student and if the family is expecting a young kid. Jeff says that when I walk through the door they are going to think their student came with their mother. Are they going to be uncomfortable with me?

The walk to school is all uphill. You climb the hill and then ascend 95 steps to the next plateau where I walk another two blocks to reach one of the ancient arched entrances to the old city. Coming from New Jersey and always having a car to go anywhere, this is a real workout. I've barely slept, having missed the plane and train, and I consider calling in sick the very first day. I talk myself out of it, but I'm really hurting.

It's the first day, and I'm overwhelmed already. I signed up for a beginners' class, but there are several people who can communicate with the instructor in Italian already. It's very intimidating until the following day when they are removed and put into an intermediate class. Still, all the instructors speak only Italian to us, and we're not allowed to speak English. How can I learn when I don't understand anything the instructors are saying?

I'm anxious for the first day to be over so I can return to my tiny bedroom and sleep, but I have a good amount of homework, and it's weighing heavy on my mind. I have only myself to blame for causing this stress. Why didn't I just chill out on a beach? I finally reach the apartment, and as soon as I walk through the door, my host tells me that Fabio called and he's driving to Siena to see me.......... Now. To compound things, instead of giving him their address, my host instructs him to meet me in front of the church. That means I need to turn around and go back up the hill and the 95 steps. I can't believe my ears!

Even though I have no romantic feelings for him, I enjoy his friendship. He has been incredibly kind to me from the beginning. As exhausted as I am, I make my way to the church, and within a few minutes, I see my friend approaching with the biggest smile. I'm suddenly happy to see him, but I can't believe he has taken it upon himself to call my host family and just show up on the very day I arrive. We take a scenic ride through the hills of Siena in his BMW and stop for cappuccino, me, my friend, Fabio, and my Italian dictionary.

During school, we get a 15-minute break on the beautiful terrace overlooking the city at 10:30 every morning. By this time, I really need a break. If I have the correct amount of Euro, I can buy a cappuccino from the vending machine that comes in a paper cup the size you get at the dentist office. My head is spinning; did I bite off more than I can chew? During the break, if the instructors hear you speaking English, they insist you stop. Sometimes I'm so frustrated in class I'm forced to speak English just to be understood. I want to scream; I'm so lost. It's 1970 all over again!

The second part of each school day is her asking us individually something in Italian in front of the class and us responding in Italian. When that's over, we are required to speak Italian to each other. I understand the idea of complete immersion into the culture, but I need much more help. Some of the students hire private tutors, but I can't afford that, too. Had I known what to expect, I would have booked less time and hired a tutor as well. It's not as if I'm attending for credits and I need to get a passing grade, but I want desperately to start speaking Italian. I thought that living with a host family would be of more help, but I'm not learning anything new with them. It's difficult getting beyond the basic pleasantries at dinner. The students that are living and going to school together are practicing on each other, and they seem to be doing the best in the class. They are picking it up quicker and finding it much easier than I am.

By the third week, I hire a young Swiss woman, enrolled in an advanced class, and pay her 10 Euro an hour for an hour a day. We meet at the park and practice. It's a perfect place, close to the school, and there's always so many people passing through from all over the world it seems. I sit on a bench alone, and before long, some Italian, usually a man, sits next to me. They inevitably start a conversation, and I explain in Italian that I'm here for six weeks to study Italian. They are always surprised when I say "*sei settimane*," six weeks, and think I mean six months. I correct them and they're shocked. It's not that I've suddenly become fluent in Italian, it's just that I know just so many words, and I repeat the same things over and over again. At least school has taught me to pronounce things well enough that most people understand what I say.

I'll never sound Italian, but being understood is all anyone needs to do. They are all so certain, too, that I'm holding back and that I really know far more than I'm letting on. It's the furthest thing from the truth! I keep telling them that even though I can speak a little, I do not understand one word when a person responds. *Niente*, nothing.

After some weeks, I venture to the park and speak Italian to anyone who will listen. It doesn't even phase me that I may be making an ass of myself. Who would have thought I'd become a babbling fool in Siena? But what a place to be a fool!

The other students are of all ages, all European or American. Many of them are living together in the same apartment or have rooms with families like I do. Some even have to take a bus in. I wasn't willing to ride a bus to school at this age. I've been invited to meet some classmates after dinner, but I'm so exhausted from lack of sleep that I don't want to make the climb up the hill and the stairs again that day. The other Americans have already formed a clique. I'm not interested in hearing about how a classmate picked up some young Italian guy and nearly immediately after meeting they are "hooking up" on a regular basis. Don't they know they give us Americans a bad name? Even if they do, they don't care, and they don't mind talking about it either.

Two German women in class befriend me. Only one speaks English, and if they hear me speak it, they correct me. That's the discipline we hear about. After a few weeks, we are able to communicate enough that we go to visit the Sienese gardens together. The English speaking woman insists that if I return to Europe I must stay with her. She has an apartment over her home I can use for free, and we'd practice Italian every day. I don't know anything about Germany's geography, but if I make it back to Italy, I'd certainly like to cross the Alps and take her up on this offer. She's genuinely kind to me, and I could be speaking Italian much better in a few weeks with her discipline. A very nice offer, indeed.

I arrive back at the apartment, and I'm told that Fabio wants me to meet him at the church again. I wish I could speak Italian and be able to communicate with him directly so I'd have the option of saying no. But I climb the hill and make the stairs again and wait - and wait. Is it possible I misunderstood? Finally, I call his cell from a public phone. When he answers, I ask, "*Dove sei?*" where are you? I don't know how to ask much else. He replies: "*a casa,*" at home. Loudly I reply, "*A casa?*" There's a few more words he says, but none of them understood by me. It's obvious he's not alone. I hang up and return to my apartment. We would never speak or write again.

On Sunday morning, I am happy driving to Jenny's to spend the day riding and eating lunch with a group of horse riders. I'm clothed in my normal riding attire, but instead of a traditional white cotton blouse, I'm wearing my new powder blue suede halter top. I thought it would be the coolest outfit for this occasion. By the time I arrive, everyone is getting a horse assigned to them. We are going out in two different groups according to skill level. I'm riding out with one of Jenny's instructors and a few other Italian women who speak no English. At least I can communicate with our guide. We are all lined up in formation, and when we reach a large clearing, the guide informs us we are going to begin our first canter. With that, I rise out of my saddle and get into my two-point position. As soon as I extend my arms to lean against the horse's neck, the snaps on my halter top pop, and my top falls to my waist. I'm no Lady Godiva, but I'm riding bareback! The Italian woman in back of me couldn't speak a word of

English, but I clearly understood her hysterical laughter. She was laughing so hard, it was difficult for her to stay on her horse.

There is still a week left before I finish with school and leave this stunning city. While planning my trip, I had seen an advertisement online for a hot air balloon ride over Tuscany that I have been fantasizing about. This is the way I want to celebrate my accomplishments with Dad. I had done the impossible with so little for the love of a parent. While heading back to the house from school, I see an office that arranges all kinds of activities, and one of them is hot air ballooning. From their brochure, I recognize it's the same company I saw online. He tells me the cost for a basket that can hold four people and the pilot is 1,500 Euros. He doesn't have anyone else at this time but he expects to book soon and to check back in a few days. When I mention the balloon ride to a fellow classmate, she expresses interest as well. I'm optimistic we'll actually get a balloon up.

By the end of the week, my classmate backs out of the ride. I return to the office, and he, too, tells me that he has no one else. My celebratory dream is now deflated. I can't justify spending 1500 Euro considering I'm planning on buying Dad's home, and I don't even have a job yet either. As I go to exit his office, a woman walks in. He tells her why I'm there, and she thinks another pilot might do it for one person at one-fourth the price. He has a small basket, even though he'd surely squeeze four people into it, but he doesn't have any other customers, and he'll take me up for 350 Euros. The only difference is he's not giving me strawberries and champagne during the flight. For 1150 Euros less, I'll buy him the champagne and strawberries. I'll help blow the balloon up, too! My mind tells me Dad is pulling some strings upstairs. Thank you, Jesus; thank you, Dad!

Saturday morning arrives, and I'm up before dawn. I climb the hill and the 95 stairs to meet *"la pilota,"* the pilot, in front of the church. No one wants to pick me up at the home! He arrives in a van with a helper, and I'm expecting he's taking me to the site where the balloon is just waiting for us to jump in, and up we'll go just like Dorothy in *The Wizard of Oz* minus a little dog. We drive into a large, commercial parking lot and park. I'm beginning to get nervous. Am I getting mugged? Who does a mugging at 6 a.m.? The three of us jump out, and the men open the van's back door, carefully removing the deflated balloon, the basket, and the large fan that inflates it. I can't believe my eyes. It's nothing like the *Wizard of Oz*. It all fit into the back of the van.

The two men very carefully start to unfold the delicate balloon, and after a while, I'm assisting with the fan and blowing it up. Just when it's ready, Maximilian, my handsome pilot, tells me to hop in. There's no ladder, just a hole in the basket to use as a step. Within seconds, we are ascending into the heavens on this gorgeous Spring morning. Just like my dream - only better!

Ascending in the balloon brings me back to my helicopter ride in 1970 when Mom dropped me off at Newark Airport. Unlike a plane that climbs at a steady pace, it goes straight up, and it feels like a supernatural power is lifting you. Nothing about it seems real or normal. We are flying far above the trees, and the thing that strikes me the most is the silence, the utter, complete lack of any sound whatsoever. The only noise is the conversation between Max and me and the swishing sound of the burner being fired up. As we're flying just north of Siena, we see the fog rise over the Chianti region. We can see for miles in both directions, and the landscape of vineyards and olive groves beneath us looks more like a painting than anything that really exists. The beauty surrounds us. I see something I've never seen before: a church attached to a home. Not a chapel, indicative of many of the large villas here, but an actual church. I think it's their rectory until I see two little kids playing in the yard. I suppose it's a Christian church, just not Roman Catholic. Or maybe the church just needed a tenant to support itself. In the tiny villages, there may be less than 15 people at a mass. I don't know how they could support itself on so few parishioners. Just heating these stone churches has to be very expensive. There's still very few people on the roads yet, and the earth seems to be perfectly still except for us. The air is chilly, but the heat from the burner feels like a breath of warm air from heaven each time he releases the flame. The swishing sound is music to my ears. I imagine what it will look like in a few weeks when the poppies are in full bloom and blanketing the beautiful landscape. August will bring the fields of sunflowers that are blessed by the blazing Summer sun, but I won't be anywhere near to experience it. I'll leave much before it gets nearly that hot.

As we start to descend, I hear the sound of dogs barking continuously. Max explains that the pitch of the swishing sound drives them crazy. He has a plan to land in a specific area where he's told his helper to meet us with the van, but when we approach the location, he is afraid to land with the high wires. The total amount of time given for each balloon ride is 40 minutes, and we've already exceeded that. I'd be happy to stay up all day. Next to cantering through the vineyards, I can't decide which is the most exciting thing I've ever done. They've both exceeded my dreams.

We are dropping lower and lower as he's moving away from the designated area into more farmland, and Max is concerned about where he's going to land. As we get closer to the ground, he says to me, "Now, don't jump out." Don't jump out? Are you kidding me? I didn't come up here to commit suicide today. He tells me we'll come in on an angle, unlike the way we've lifted, and that he'll jump on the one side to tilt the basket as we're touching down. It's becoming a little more frightening to me, but I'm definitely not going to jump!

We're drifting closer and closer to the ground, and we are headed for an olive grove in the village of Uopini when I suddenly get a feeling of *deja vu* when we stopped to have a picnic lunch on a farmer's property and he went absolutely crazy on us. Now we are landing our balloon on someone else's property in the middle of someone's olive grove. Maybe I should jump! We are getting closer and closer, and I see that we are going to land where this farmer has planted new olive trees. We're going to kill his new trees!

Incredibly, the basket lands perfectly between two new trees, but the deflated balloon was stuck on the branches. The farmer comes out running with his family behind him, yelling, and I'm frightened of what he may do. As it turns out, they are all actually very excited to see us and happy to have us land on their property. A first for them, too. He ran to get his ladder, and they very gently removed the balloon. Not one branch was damaged.

Once school is completed, I begin the next four weeks at different *agriturismi,* all unique, one week each. The first is a lovely home west of the Chianti region where a single woman originally from the United States has a riding facility. When I arrive, I discover that she will not canter, but she tells me she could arrange with a friend to take me out with his horses and canter. I don't care who owns the horses; I only care that I can do more than just walk or trot. The bedrooms are very nice, but the bathroom is not en suite. Another fact I missed. Now I understand why this facility is so reasonable compared to all the others. Only for two days does she have other guests, and the bathroom is more than enough to accommodate several people at a time.

The following morning I wake up with a fever and am bed ridden for nearly the entire week. I attribute it to the stress and the rainy and shivering cold weather nearly the entire four weeks of school. I never do get to horseback ride. When I think I am feeling a little better, I go to a local village to take in the sites, but after an hour or so, I feel the fever rising again. Back in bed I go.

The next week is spent at a converted monastery just 15 minutes south of Siena in a small village called S. Rocco a Pilli. The apartments are spread out over the beautiful property, immaculately manicured, all one story, attached units. The entire complex is shaped like two horseshoes with picturesque courtyards between them. Some people just came to relax here, and others use it as a home base to see all the stunning villages in the Chianti region. It's enchanting.

My apartment is perfect. A small, functional kitchen, a dining room with a wooden table long enough to accommodate far more than this apartment would sleep (I assume it must have been what the priests actually used when it was a monastery), a nice bedroom, and the most unusual bathroom that was probably a small wine cellar because you walk down five steps and enter through an arched doorway. The tiny shower is in the far end, and there are no windows being underground like this. My first reaction is it feels like I am going to prison each time I go to the bathroom, but then I get used to it. I keep the door open because it still spooks me.

The courtyards make it comfortable and easy to meet your neighbors. An older woman is here with her husband and tells me that she likes to travel around the small villages like I do, but her husband prefers to sit and read on the grounds. We agree to visit thermal springs the following day together that I had seen in a brochure and made several inquires in an attempt to find where it's actually located. It's still warm enough to go swimming, and this particular thermal bath happens to be free. We drive to the place, park the car, and as we're walking, we see several very old vans and tens of people in the baths. From the top, I see there are tiers of natural bathtubs with several people soaking in each. The springs are famous for helping skin diseases, and from a distance, I can see how badly afflicted some people are. As it turns out, it's not a place I want to be bathing and relaxing after all! My friend stays at the top, and I make my way to the very bottom of the spring that's the size of a small lake. But the bottom is full of stones and painful to walk on. I had driven all this way because the photographs were so stunning I had to experience it.   I should have known better than to expect a different crowd. The operative word was "free."

My third *agriturismo* is a stunning 17th century villa in Rapolano Terme, exactly like the ones that grace the covers of the Tuscan calendars. The red, vibrant poppies are in full bloom now and are brilliantly thriving over the stunning landscape. Driving past the old stone entrance up the long, cypress lined driveway to the main villa is stunning in itself. The young owner escorts me to my room on the second floor by entering through a set of 20-foot doors on the first floor. Even the skeleton keyhole is enormous. In order for me to shut the door, I need to get on the first step and extend my body to grab the handle and slam it shut.   As you climb the high, stone staircase, you enter through the double doors, everything is double doors, into the common living room with an enormous fireplace; its firebox five feet high alone. My room is the first one on the left, double doors, of course, and

161

opens to a large, gorgeous bedroom with a fresco adorning the domed ceiling. My white tiled en suite bathroom is large and modern and has a circular shower of clear glass. My favorite feature is the heated towel racks.

Breakfast is served in the kitchen each morning just past the living room, and I seem to be the only one there most mornings. And then I realize that I am the only one in the villa many of the nights, and that frightens me. I lock myself in my room and turn up Frank Sinatra. Thank God for Frank! I'd be all alone otherwise.

I'm told there are two good restaurants in the immediate area. I have dinner at one my first night, but when I try the second restaurant the following day, I eat there every night until I leave six days later. They don't offer a menu until I ask, and I can tell that the owner is very uncomfortable with me being alone. In Italy, the men frequently dine with their friends and maybe alone, especially a widower, but a woman eating solo is unusual, unless a tourist, of course. But this is not a large tourist area, and the customers are local residents that he serves all the time. He cannot even look at me. I wait for quite some time to be served after waiting to just take my order. Their food is so good and so reasonably priced, I keep returning. During these long periods of waiting at the table, I always have my notebook, and I'm normally writing to Dad's attorney. In the end, the letter is 15 pages detailing the last eight years.

During the day, I visit the local villages like Asciano, Sinalunga, Buonconvento, and Lucignano. With a gift from Debbie and Jeanne, I spend the day at the beautiful L'Antica Querciolaia Fonte Termale in Rapolano Terme where I get a massage and swim in their beautiful thermal pools located inside and out.

The last place I stay before heading south is at yet another *agriturismo* close to Cortona where *Under the Tuscan Sun* was filmed. The manager keeps expressing his interest in me and keeps inviting me to go out with him and a few of the other guests. The accommodations include dinner, so the guests get to know each other during their stay while eating whatever the host cooks that day and listening to classical music. He keeps asking me to accompany him to an opera, and I keep refusing, mostly because I am deathly afraid of his driving. But he keeps asking, and eventually I give in. The opera is to be held on Torre del Largo immediately across from Puccini's home, outdoors in this magnificent setting, and it's the 100th anniversary of his famous opera, *Madam Butterfly*. I don't know opera, but I know this is a big deal. We secure my ticket, and I'm not sitting anywhere near him. I actually have a better seat just 20 rows from the front of the stage. The young couple seated to my right engage me in conversation when I see a woman walking down an aisle 15 feet away from me holding a man's hand, and I realize it's Andrea Bocelli. I may not know opera, but I adore Andrea. Another stunning night in Tuscany.

I don't understand one word of the opera, but I love the ambience, the costumes, and I love watching all the old men in the audience singing every word. They've probably been raised on opera like I was on Sinatra. To be in this magnificent setting across the street from Puccini's actual home on this lake on this incredible night just 15 feet away from Andrea is truly a gift that doesn't go unnoticed, and we arrive back at the *agriturismo* safely.

The manager continues trying to convince me into staying; he'll give me a deal he says. But I know there's no free lunch. I don't want to hurt his feelings and keep telling him my three-month stay on my passport is up. He has other plans for me, trying to convince me in various ways. "All of this could be yours," he says. He goes on to tell me how he was raised in the South and how he came upon this property. A whole long story, too, about the closing on the property. When that doesn't work, he says it could be a platonic relationship and we'd speak only Italian so I'd learn. It's becoming a consideration.............. until I walk down to see the farm animals in their pens. I don't understand why they are following me, squealing loudly, as I walk from side to side. I'm told later that the farmhand is out today, and then it dawns on me the following morning that the reason they were so anxious with me was because they were hungry. No one fed them, and the owner/manager didn't care enough to do it. Now, there isn't a snowball's chance in hell I am staying - even if he pays me!

I'm eating alone in a small restaurant, and there are two women dining next to me that strike up a conversation. The first question is always the same: "Where are you from?"

I reply, "The United States. And, you?"

"Germany," she replies. " Is this your first trip to Italy?"

"No, this is my seventh time here. Have you ever been to the United States?" I continue.

"No, and I never would," she says emphatically.

I'm taken aback and **make the mistake of asking,** "Why?"

Then I have to hear that President Bush started a war...........on and on. I respond by telling her that we didn't go into Iraq alone; we went in with Tony Blair. Why isn't this bitch hating the English? Never said a damn word about them. I turn my head and never look back.

As anxious as I was to complete my Italian course with all the stress it was causing me, I make the surprising decision to return to Scuola Leonardo da Vinci instead of going to the South for two weeks. Since I've been gone for four weeks and haven't practiced nearly enough, I've forgotten a great deal of it already. This time I'll share an apartment with three other students. How bad can it be?

As it turns out, I'm only one block away from that little, uncomfortable shoebox of a room I had just four weeks ago. This means I still have to climb the same hill and the same 95 stairs to school each day. I'm almost used to this now. The apartment has four bedrooms, and I have the largest one by far. The other students are not happy about it and want to know why "I" got it. We share a bathroom and a small kitchen. Two of my roommates are young Asian women enrolled in a different school that seem to come from wealth, and the other roommate is an American in her late twenties. The Asian women speak no English, and the only thing I understand is when they scold me for putting something on "their" shelf in the refrigerator. I didn't know we had our own shelves........................ bitch. *Capisci?*

The American woman dashes out every morning to meet up with another classmate even though we are in the same class and never invites me to join them. I guess I don't fit in; probably too old. She doesn't know me nearly well enough to dislike me; we've just met and rarely spoke. She asks if I have plans for the weekend, and I tell her no. I have a car and she wants to know if we could do something together outside of the city. "Sure." She says there's a chance her friends are coming to meet her, and only in that case would she have to postpone. Friday comes and suddenly she hears from her friends and is now cancelling. Ok, no problem; I'm not sitting home; I'm the one with the car.

Monday morning the instructor goes around the room and asks everyone what they did. I'm not close to being fluent in Italian, but as a few students speak, I'm able to understand that they were the "friends" my roommate was referring to, and not people that were driving into Siena to pick her up as she said. I am beyond furious. Not because I wasn't invited, but how she tried to use me. All she had to do was be honest, but instead, she chose to lie.

With the mess I have at home, fighting years with my siblings, the last thing I want is a confrontation with someone in Italy. Why would I get so upset? Because I've reached my limit with people attempting to take advantage of me. I'm infuriated, and I can't let it slide. I don't know how I will respond; I just know I am going to go off on her like a rocket if I see her soon, and chances are I will.

The following morning I climb the hill, and I see her at the top of the stairs. My heart is racing, and now the Jersey Girl inside of me is pushing to get out. She turns as if to say hello, and I slam her with my mouth. She doesn't know what hit her; she can't even respond. All I can remember saying is, "Who do you think you're trying to make a fool of?"

That night there's a note under my bedroom door from her saying that she didn't mean to mislead me and that because we are roommates and classmates and because the school is so small, she wants to make amends. She's inviting me out Friday night with a few other friends. I don't want to go, but I don't want to look bad to the others, either. At least there are several other Americans I can socialize with.

The last two weeks of school is finally completed, and I'm heading to my last stop, Rome, before returning home. The other three roommates are remaining. Actually, the American has no intentions of returning to the States, and she thinks she'll learn enough Italian, get a job, and become an Italian even without a drop of Italian blood in her. I can't get away from the three of them fast enough.

One of my classmates has decided to take the train to Rome with me and stay for the weekend before returning to school. I find an apartment online in historic Rome, right where I want to be. She will be a great help considering I added two more pieces of luggage since I arrived with all my new leather bags, shoes, boots, and scarves I purchased for everyone.

The bus finally arrives in Rome, and we catch a taxi to our apartment on Via Giulia. When we reach the entrance to the street, I'm stunned at its beauty with its elegant arch dripping long foliage that spans its entire length. Then our driver informs us it's a one-way in the other direction, but once he leaves, we realize that it was just easier for him to leave us at the foot of the road. We drag all my luggage up this beautiful street for a half a mile in the heat.

We reach our small apartment on the first floor of the building facing Via Giulia. My guest will sleep on the sofa, and I have a bed in the loft. There's a small bathroom, and the kitchen is so tiny that the table folds up into the wall when not in use. The entire apartment consists of one window - yes, one window! The ad for the apartment says there is air conditioning, but we soon learn it's clearly a mistake. That's a big mistake if you hate the heat like I do. And what about the traffic noise living on this busy cobblestone street and you can't close the window? We have no choice but to keep the one window open day and night, but the cars driving over the cobblestones make it sound like they're in my very apartment. There's no escaping it.

My friend is not Catholic, and I tell her that I'm going to the Vatican in the morning and be blessed by the Pope in the Vatican's Square. Surprisingly, she wants to come along. She's leaving to go back to Siena today, and in a few days, I'm returning home. The dread of returning to an empty home is building up, and I'm getting sadder and sadder each passing moment. The only thing my mind is saying to do is go to Navona. I didn't know about this famous piazza for many years, but since I've discovered it, it was all I talked to Dad about and would excitedly tell him about us returning to Italy. I'd always say the same thing: "Dad, we're going to Rome, and we're going to eat and dance in Navona, Dad, you and me; we'll eat and dance in Navona." A dream in this glorious city; a city he grew to love, too. I imagined us eating a very expensive meal in the center of it all and people watch for hours. We'd never get bored there. Dad would look at me and just nod his head in agreement. It was always about Navona.

Dad had this funny wave, regal-like, and I always called it the clown wave. I never saw anyone do it before, and I don't remember it as a child. He must have picked it up after he retired when you have time to do strange things. If nothing else, it was adorable, almost his signature. So when Pope John Paul II waved to us from his balcony with the thousands of people below cheering *papa'*, without any forethought whatsoever I raise my hand and give him Ray's clown wave. It's as if my father is moving my arm.

The tears roll down my face no matter how hard I try and contain myself. I keep thinking about returning home and facing the music with attorneys, and there's my biggest fear of not being able to qualify to buy Dad's home. My friend boards her bus, and I walk back to my tiny apartment and cry my eyes out. I don't think anything in the world would lift my spirits today, but I need to push myself. I need to get to Navona.

After all the crying, it's dusk, and the piazzas are not nearly as crowded. People are home cooking or waiting to go out to eat, many of the shops are closed except for gelato, and dinnertime doesn't start till eight. I enter Navona from a side street, not where I normally come in, and I see how empty it is in comparison to all my regular visits; a little surreal, I think. I immediately notice the human statues working around the large fountain closest to me that are dressed in costumes and appear eight feet tall while standing on a box hidden by their skirt. Their faces are painted white, you cannot tell if they are male or female, and they are wearing these outrageously large hats, making them appear even that much taller. The statues are expressionless. Suddenly, one of them sees me approaching from the narrow cobblestone road flowing into Navona, and what he does next takes my breath away: he looks directly at me, picks his hand up and gives me Ray's clown wave!

Dad was already there; he beat me to Navona!!

***

When I arrived home, all the perennials in front of the house were in full bloom, and I had been gone long enough that I didn't remember which key opened my front door. Richard, Debbie and Jeanne were there to welcome me home, and my happiness came in giving them their Italian gifts. Angela was still living in my basement, but our friendship greatly deteriorated. She no longer needed me; she had her new boyfriend. Cousin Joe was still on the second floor, and Rose continued to stop in frequently.

I accepted a part-time job with FedEx working evenings while I tried to decide what I would do permanently. As I drove down the long, flat road approaching the building, I fantasized about riding down on horseback and ached for Italy. I couldn't put my own home up for sale either until the estate was settled. I remained in limbo.

I was grateful to God for helping me achieve my goals and for the time I had with Dad, but I missed him terribly! I'd do it all over again. And I never referred to him as Ray anymore; it was no longer necessary. He will forever be just Dad!

Chapter Eight

I'M LIVING WITH HITLER'S NEIGHBORS

Life at Home: 2004-2005

It's Christmastime, and I am becoming more despondent without Dad during this holiday season. His estate is not nearly settled, and the war of the siblings rages on. So, I decide to run to Italy for two more months. By the time I return, Jeff will surely have everything settled. I've known from the very first day I returned home with Dad that I had no intentions of ever leaving my childhood home again. This is home; this is where I once had a family; it will always be home.

Before I leave for Italy, I surprise even myself and extend an olive branch to one of my sisters, the one who never attended Dad's funeral. We hadn't gotten along very well most of our lives, and our differences escalated over the years when I resented the way she was treating both of our parents, especially Mom who was handicapped by this time. I want to let the hatred go, so I'm "gifting" her Mom's diamond. All three of us had wanted it when Mom passed, but I was the only one who could afford to buy it from the estate. Mom confided in me just before she passed that she wanted me to "get" it because she didn't know if the others would sell it. But when I told her if she felt that strongly she should just leave it to me, she quickly replied, "I can't do that; you'll have to fight for it." That would be the first and last time she'd tell me to fight with my sisters.

I'm already willing Mom's ring to her daughter, but now I'm giving my sister use of the ring until her child turns 25. The ring has been sitting in my safe deposit box since Mom passed in 1988, a waste of God's beauty. I can't think of a better olive branch!

The night before I leave for Italy, I put the ring in a box with a small replica of Michelangelo's Pieta' and drive to Aunt Dee's house, whom I still have no relationship with. I leave it with her daughter with the only instructions to give it to my sister. She cannot believe what I'm saying and keeps questioning me, making sure she got the instructions correct. No one knows the content of the box except me, Debbie, and Jeanne who are with me. They think I'm nuts. They don't understand how I could get beyond her not attending his funeral. I just think this is what my parents would want. Even in death, I want to make them happy.

***

I have another wild schedule these coming two months, and aside from going horseback riding with Jenny for a few days and visiting Maria and her family at the pig farm for a week, I'll spend New Year's in Rome. After the Feast of the Epiphany in the beginning of January, I'll take my friend's invitation and go to Germany and practice Italian with her. After riding with Jenny, I've found another riding center in a different part of Tuscany with a great apartment. I explain why I want to be there for Christmas, and I learn that the owner, Nadia, has just recently lost her mom as well, and for that reason, she agrees to take me Christmas week. Her husband will be my trainer. I could never get this training in the States due to our litigious nature, so I'm going to take advantage of every day I can learn from him, and I'll make the most of Christmas for what it's all about - Christ! With Christ in my heart, I already have Christmas.

On Christmas Eve, Nadia invites me to dinner at her home, just the three of us, and then go for a late night walk through the village. Every main piazza in the villages has stacked their wood piles exactly the same for this night when the people of the town go from church to church admiring the Nativity scenes they have created that year. Outside people are offering free warm cups of wine to passersby's in tiny paper cups as we walk between the churches. Warm wine - that's a first. At midnight, a procession begins down the main street in celebration of the birth of Christ. We don't stay for the procession, and Nadia and I make plans to go to the Abbey of Sant'Antimo near Montalcino the following morning. The Abbey is considered one of Italy's most beautiful Romanesque churches dating back to the 9th century and was one of the most powerful monasteries around Siena in the Middle Ages. Christmas is turning out to be beautiful.

As our car winds through the Tuscan hills, you see how majestic The Abbey truly is, standing alone in the valley surrounded by vineyards and fields and one, single cypress tree. We are seated in the nave, and what strikes me is the small number of people attending the mass. With its history, I expected it would be packed. But we are in an area where the land is primarily agricultural, and there are more farm animals than people. Nadia and I sit through mass, and my favorite part is when we offer a sign of peace to each other. I grab her hand and say, "*pace,*" peace, and kiss on the cheek. Just as we approach the priest for communion, Nadia, standing in front of me, starts to cry hysterically. We both receive communion, and I wrap my arm around her, and together, side by side, we walk back to our pew. The first Christmas after her loss overtook her emotions at that moment.

I can't believe the difference in how Italians decorate for Christmas compared to the Americans. Coming from the country of the Pope, I'd expect nearly everything to be lit up and Nativity scenes everywhere. I'm so wrong. Instead of a Santa Claus, they have Babbo Natale, or Father Christmas, who is a skinnier and more regal looking version of Santa Claus. Instead of Mrs. Claus, they have Befana, also called the Christmas Witch, an old woman who delivers gifts to children throughout Italy on Epiphany Eve (the night of January 5th) in a similar way to St. Nicholas or Santa Claus. Befana is usually portrayed as an old lady riding a broomstick through the air wearing a black shawl and is covered in soot because, like Santa, she enters the children's houses through the chimney. She is often smiling and carries a bag or hamper filled with candy, gifts, or both. As I pass through the villages, *Babbo Natale* is often seen at a table outside a restaurant drinking wine to attract customers. On some homes, his skinny body is splattered against the side of the home. To my surprise, there are very few Christmas lights or any decorations adorning the homes.

Nadia's husband Piero is somewhat of a genuine horse whisperer. Nadia tells me of his accomplishments with a young lady who had never ridden any horse until he met her just two years ago and how she recently took second place in a dressage competition. I know how incredibly lucky I am to have such a trainer, and I'm a little nervous. How much will be expected of me? Will he get annoyed with my abilities? How will this week end? I tell him I'm here to canter into his part of the woods, and when he puts me on a horse the first day, he informs me that he thinks it's better that I take lessons instead of riding out into the countryside. When he asks how many lessons I've had, I tell him about 50, but because of the way I'm riding, he tells me that they were babysitting me. Ouch! I had been taking my riding lessons so seriously and constantly pushing the trainer to teach me more, and now the truth has struck me in the face. They were treating me like a child no matter how much I paid and continued to push them. But this is why I'm here now, to learn at an aggressive pace. I tell him my goal is to jump, and he's got one week. It's almost funny. I appreciate his honesty and am only concerned with achieving my goal of jumping. I'm not expecting three feet; one foot would make me very happy.

Each day I get on the horse in the ring, and after ten minutes, I feel like the horse is riding me. Piero is really pushing me. I'm doing things I've never seen people taking lessons do, like taking my feet out of the stirrups while riding, but then I remember he knows exactly what he's doing. When I tell him I can't do something, he tells me I'm wrong and pushes me. He's always right. As each day passes, I'm doing new things to strengthen my legs and balance myself in the saddle. The only thing I cannot come to terms with is he insists there is no cantering, just a slower gallop. I'm deathly afraid of galloping on an English saddle, but he insists. The ring feels smaller and smaller making the turns. Within a few days, he starts taking out the poles to jump over. Even just walking over them on horseback is scary at first; it's not a smooth gait at all. But that doesn't deter me from wanting to jump. Each day there are more poles he places in different positions. Before the end of the week, he has me jumping a good foot or more. Each jump is so frightening that I now close my eyes when the horse makes the jump. Who does that? Nuts do that. But I'm still not deterred from my goal.

Piero tells me to start at one end of the ring with a trot, go into a gallop, and then before I complete the circle, jump. Now we are combining two of the most frightening things before I make one complete turn around the ring. I'm more nervous about the gallop than the jump, and when he yells for me to jump, I get my instructions mixed up and lean backwards instead of forward, and down I go. I'm embarrassed, but happy I'm not hurt. The horse is tall, and I've fallen about five feet right on my back. I quickly get up, and Piero thinks I'm going to stop for the day. Instead, I brush myself off and get right back in the saddle. By the end of the week, he says something I never imagined he'd ever say to me: "You're actually pretty good." I can only imagine what he could teach me if I could stay a few months.

I arrive at the pig farm, and Maria is so happy to see me. Her arms are reaching out to greet me yelling, "Debbie, Debbie, Debbie." Angelo is just smiling at the two of us. She's the only one I regularly speak Italian to, and even with my limited vocabulary, she understands me. We are friends. I'm staying in the same unit with the tiny spiral staircase because it has the best views and it's the least expensive. It's just adorable. My only problem I have is getting the fire started in the fireplace. The wood is cut and stored immediately next to my unit, but it's always damp. I'd never survive as a camper.

Maria's restaurant has more partygoers celebrating Christmas. Aside from me, there is only one other table tonight, a bunch of male coworkers, no women. They occupy three tables that are set up to create one long one. All the men are extremely cordial all evening even after all the wine they're drinking, and the men seated closest to me continue to offer me wine all night. They try to include me in a conversation several times, but we can barely communicate. As each one rises to leave and says *Buon Natale* to each other, they pass and stop to kiss me, too. It is all so sweet...... until we come to the very last one. As he follows the others' lead saying good-bye to me, he, too, comes over and kisses me on the cheek. With that, he proceeds to ask me in Italian if I am interested in going to bed with him. He wants to stay and return to my room! Just like that, as casual as if he was saying hello. I turn my head as if he doesn't exist. He didn't deserve any response.

After the guys leave and Maria is cleaning up, I'm able to tell her what he asked me. I don't even know if she is going to understand what I'm trying to tell her, but she does, and she is dumbfounded! She carries on as if she caught us in the act, and all I can do is laugh. Angelo wants to know what's going on by the way she's reacting, and when she tells him, he turns to her and jokingly asks his wife if he can go to her bed tonight. Maria is mortified - but hysterically laughing. Now I'm laughing at them.

I tell Maria where I stayed last year and how surprised I was that the farm is very near hers. I tell her how the "owner" was interested in me and wanted me to stay longer. He went as far as to say "this place could be yours." Maria shocks me with the news that he is not even the owner of the farm, just the manager. The same farm that he told me this detailed story how he found it and how he came to purchase it. I think she misunderstands me, but both she and her husband assure me he never owned it and that they know all the farmers in the area. I'm sure he never thought as an American I'd ever learn the truth.

Before the week is up, Maria and Angelo leave for the very first time in 25 years to celebrate their silver anniversary with a cruise. Her sons are finally old enough to run the place in their absence. The restaurant stays open, and I'm always well fed by the kids.

My phone rings while I'm in bed. I'm shocked that someone from home could actually reach me so deep in the mountains. I've been getting text messages from my good friend, Frank, every day, but no calls. It's Mom's sister, Aunt Dee, calling. We haven't spoken since the funeral; she hadn't been home the day I dropped the package off for my sister. She tells me that she had called my sister to tell her she has a package from me, but my sister doesn't want it. She's asking me if she should throw it away. I nearly croak. She asks, "What's in it? The Hope Diamond?" Strange choice of words, I think. "Well, nearly." I explain what it is and why, but Aunt Dee is still shocked knowing I paid for it. I tell her Dad is gone, I didn't lose the house, and he was able to stay with me to the very end. All three of us were getting the exact same inheritance. They had nothing to be jealous about. Had I done what they wanted and sold his home eight years ago, they wouldn't be getting one dime now.

The following day I receive another call from Aunt Dee telling me that my sister was so certain it was something in the box that would enrage her, and now that she knows it's Mom's diamond, she wants to pick it up today. But Dee told her that she isn't giving it to her without speaking to me first. She became enraged, so much so, that she went on a rant for over an hour fighting with her to release it. But Dee won't. When I hear how she treated my aunt, I tell Dee that if she wants it now, there would be conditions attached to it. I'd write up something, fax it over to Jeff when I reached a nearby village, and she'd have to sign it. Without that signature, she isn't getting it. Now, I'm really pissed. I knew she could easily be a hateful bitch to anyone in our immediate family, but I never expected that she'd treat Mom's sister this way. I tell Dee that I will handle it with the attorney and she needn't have to deal with my sister again. It isn't her problem - except for the fact that she has physical possession of the diamond.

I fax the agreement to the attorney stating the conditions: she cannot bad mouth my parents to anyone anymore; the ring could be used by her, but not changed, until her daughter reaches the age of 25; she has to tell her daughter where it came from; and lastly, I want a photo of the kids at least once a year.

Jeff phones soon after receiving the fax. My sister was more than anxious to get it that she kept phoning him. When she didn't get a response fast enough, she had another attorney call. All Jeff said to me was that she wanted to make a change to the agreement, and without asking what change, I quickly say absolutely not. I was still willing to just hand over this 1 3/4 carat diamond after this display with our aunt, and she wants to make a change? I never give Jeff a chance to say one more word, and the deal is off the table. She screwed herself out of something she really wanted - and was getting it for free! But now I know it played out this way for a reason: My mom wants the ring to remain with me.

On to Jenny's for a few days to ride through the vineyards. It's become an obsession; once in a lifetime all of a sudden is not nearly enough. It's the only thing I truly love to do. Jenny always talks about how so many of her guests from the United States keep returning. As soon as they go home, they start saving for their next riding vacation there. I can see why. But I like to see more of Tuscany, and Jenny doesn't have the only riding center in the region. I must admit, the rides are glorious, and the food is a close second.

Jenny and Pietro greet me warmly. Pietro is really up there in age and moves slowly. When we return to the house on horseback, he's often sitting on the porch, as if waiting for us. It's a face I know and I'm always happy to see when I arrive. I get a big hello; he remembers me, too. I didn't know if I'd ever have the guts to ask to ride with Jenny again after falling twice in one day. I didn't think she'd ever want me to return. But to my surprise, she accepts me back. I won't be doing the same ride, not even close, but we'll still be cantering through the same landscape minus the brush. Perfect! This trip I get a larger room because there are no other overnight guests. They even leave me alone on the farm one day, as if I'm a permanent tenant. It's weird to have the farm to myself; I'm so out of my element. But I feel amongst friends here.

Our rides are beautiful, so, so beautiful. On Sundays, Jenny has local riders join us, and her son usually has friends that come for dinner. There's always a great mix of people at the table from all over Europe and the United States, and it's never boring. We eat what they make; it's not a restaurant. If you don't like a course, there's another, and no one ever leaves unsatisfied. And there's always Chianti wine.

My next stop is historic Rome. I've found a bed and breakfast not far from Piazza Navona and close to the Tiber River where I can pass over the bridge into Trastevere, which is always jumping in the evenings, within minutes. When I had been to Navona last and the human statue gave me Dad's clown wave, I knew Dad was still with me, and I stood there stunned, frozen. There was no way anyone could possibly know what this meant except Jesus himself. As I stood there motionless, he pointed his finger directly at me, waving me over to him, and then mimed for me to take a photo with him. I knew exactly what he was saying without the words. I walked over to him standing eight feet tall and just stood next to him as he wrapped his arm around my shoulder. We stood there for some time as if I was part of his act. It didn't feel strange to me; not one moment. I felt the presence of Dad, and time stood still. People walked by and took photos of him with his arm around me, and eventually, I asked someone to take one with my camera. It was so natural; it was so Dad to send in a clown!

The space I rent for the week in Rome comes with a kitchenette minus a stove and a bedroom with a nice balcony overlooking the courtyard. And it's quiet, a major benefit in this city. The owners, two young doctors, bring me yogurt every morning for breakfast. The way the apartment is set up, you walk up to their living room, and when you reach the top of the stairs, they have a wrought iron gate to the ceiling that separates their space from mine. It's a little strange, but they are rarely in that room and always make me feel very comfortable and welcome. Living here makes me feel like a Roman.

I walk to the Vatican to see how it looks this time of year. Instead of having a Nativity scene inside the church, it is set up in St. Peter's Square, and the figures are life-sized. In Piazza Navona, *Babbo Natale* and *Befana* are there with their sleigh and are willing to take photos with anyone for 10 Euro. The piazza is filled with small vendors selling different kinds of candy that would appeal to small children, but there are no displays of toys.

My objective being here is to walk the main *strada* from Piazza Venezia to Piazza del Popolo, the original entrance to Rome, on New Year's Eve. It's a long walk, and I'm anxious to see how the Italians bring in the new year. For all I know, the party could be on the other side of town, but I'm here, and this is where my heart has been telling me to go. In my mind, it's the Italian version of Times Square, which I've never had an interest in attending on New Year's Eve. But this year it's different; everything is different.

I plan on eating dinner out before making this long walk, but except for pizza or gelato, there's no room at any restaurant on this night. As I'm walking toward Piazza del Popolo on Via del Corso, the streets are packed with pedestrians, both young and old, and Via del Corso is covered with broken glass bottles already. People are yelling *"auguri,"* best wishes, to me in the street as we pass each other. As I get closer and closer to Piazza del Popolo, I can barely get by the crowds, and I'm becoming more and more concerned with the broken glass that is increasing with each step forward. Passing one of the piazzas, I see a large, loud commotion, and walk over to check it out, but at 5'2", I can't see over the crowd. It's now five minutes to midnight. I make my way through the crowd, inching my way to the center of the excitement, and I see somewhat of a circus act, a few people riding life-sized mechanical elephants. Nearly everyone has a bottle of spirits in their hands, champagne I gather. As the clock strikes closer to 12, I'm getting sadder thinking about this past year and about starting a new year all alone. I pushed myself to be here because Dad would only want happiness for me. I'm holding back the tears somehow; I don't want anyone to notice. Why would they? They are all exuberant, and it seems I'm the only sad person in the entire city. I'm also very curious to see if they kiss each other at midnight like we do. I'm expecting they do considering all the broken bottles.

When it strikes midnight, I notice that not many people are kissing, but they are popping their corks. I look around just to take in every second of this experience I know I'll never have again, and at that moment, a very handsome, young man approaches me. He looks about 19, young enough to be my own son. He's with his friends, but he leaves them to come meet me. I'm more than double his age and wonder what could he possibly want. Actually, only to be kind. He saw a sad face in the crowd, alone, and wanted to be with me for that moment. He spoke a little English, and like me, assume he mixes his words up because he tells me what a "big" woman I am. At 118 pounds, I don't think big would describe me, but I take this as a compliment he was attempting to make. Unfortunately, there isn't much to be said between us with our lack of verbal skills, and he never came onto me physically, but I wanted to kiss him *Buon Anno*, Happy New Year. I stopped myself because, with our age difference, I felt it inappropriate and the fact that he may think I'm coming onto him. I hadn't thought of starting the new year as a cougar, but he's so handsome, maybe I should rethink this. We say our good-byes, and as he walks away, I immediately regret my decision to not kiss him on the cheek. After all, he saw a perfect stranger in the crowd and left his friends to console me. All I could think about was how lucky his mother is! My second thought: does he have a single uncle that looks like him?

The holidays are over, and I survived them. I couldn't have done it at home. I need to wait until the Feast of the Epiphany is over when my German friend's apartment would be empty. In the meantime, I'll go back to Jenny's for a few days before crossing the Alps by train into Munich. From there, I'll get another train to her home.

I'm back at Jenny's, even taking lessons in the ring with other students to fill my day. It's weird how they are giving me instructions in Italian, forgetting I really don't understand, but after a while, I begin to comprehend and actually like it. I'm assimilating. Then Jenny stuns me when she asks if I want to jump. I can't believe my ears. The same woman who almost had a heart attack when I fell twice is asking me if I want to jump! I never dreamed I'd live to hear her say this. But she has seen the difference in me and knows I'm getting better, more balanced, and now I can go out for five hours and have no problems posting the entire time. A big improvement from the time we first met! She even jokes and says we should send a photo to the people who had been riding with me back then because they, too, would never believe it.

Piero drives me to the station to catch my train to Munich, which will go through the night, and I need to change trains once before crossing the Alps. It's dark, cold, and I'm alone. I board my first train, and just as the train is about to leave one of the stations, I realize this is where I need to make my connection. But the train has started to move, and I can't go any faster with the luggage. I'm standing at the door and make the decision to throw the luggage onto the platform and then I'll jump, like I'm a stunt woman! That's where my mind goes. Luckily, one of the men working on the platform sees me and yells to the conductor to stop the train. I step off, and he assists me with my belongings. This man was my angel; he appeared at the exact moment I needed him and stayed in sight until my connection arrived.

I'm riding with five other people in the same compartment because I was told my choices were limited due to the size and amount of luggage. None of them speak any English and are not happy to be sharing their space with a stranger. As the night grows older, each one slouches down and extends their legs and rests their feet on the seat across from them. That's fine if you're family, but I'm not. I have to share this small space with this entire family all through the night like this. If I start an argument, it would only make this night worse. Morning will eventually come.

I finally reach Munich, not one moment too soon. I gather my belongings and go to the window with my friend's address in hand and show it to the clerk because I cannot pronounce it, a place called Berchtesgaden. My friend knows my train schedule and will meet me there when I arrive. I'm getting very excited now because in just a few weeks I'll be speaking Italian so much better. She'll never allow me to speak English as if we're still in school. What a great opportunity!

My train finally arrives in this town that I'll never learn how to pronounce. I've never seen such long words in my life. I wonder how they read these long street signs without getting into an accident. Are they 25 years old before they're able to read? And, unlike Italian, it's such a harsh sounding language. You'd never think they were neighbors. But having the Alps between them explains it all; they hadn't met.

I get off the train and soon see my friend. She quickly comes to greet me, and I say, "*Ciao, mia amica, come stai?*" She looks at me and says, "Oh, speak English; I've moved on." Are you serious? Now you want to speak English? She explained that she was planning her next trip to India, and Italy was out of her mind altogether. I just wish I knew this before I crossed the Alps given that practicing Italian is the reason I'm here.

We drive to her town of Berchtesgaden, and I cannot believe what a stunning place it is. A true winter wonderland in the Bavarian Alps. Even the view from my skylight in the bedroom is of the third highest mountain in the country. She and her husband take me all around this beautiful municipality. One day I spend at their ski resort, another day she and I cross country ski with her grandchildren, and then another to see their deep glacial lake, and, of course, their best known site, Eagle's Nest, Hitler's summer resort. Because of the snow, we cannot get up to see Eagle's Nest. Always the honor student, I'm embarrassed to tell them I never heard of it. I'm told that because the area is so stunning, Hitler's railroad car was made of glass on the ceiling and both sides so he could see all of this amazing landscape.

Throughout my visit, I continually hear how the Americans are too wasteful with everything, how spoiled a society we are, and how we are polluting the earth. Yes, that's true; I can't disagree. German cars are typically smaller and use less gasoline, and they walk much more than we do. Yes, you're right again. I hear her husband become more agitated as he's discussing the Americans, and then she jumps in speaking German so I don't know what is being said. By now, I have about 120 pounds of luggage, and it's not easy for me to just move around freely. Maybe I did the wrong thing by coming, but in spite of everything, except for these conversations about Americans, they are very good to me. I reciprocate their kindness by inviting them to dinner concerts and gifting her every day with something I purchased that day. Since he retired a year ago, they have a big breakfast every morning and then tea and cake every afternoon at 1 p.m. In the past year, she says she has gained 20 pounds and that it is the 1 p.m. cake that did it. I feel uncomfortable, as if I'm imposing, but they insist I join them for each meal when I'm here. I never was a big cake eater, but suddenly I'm in search of the best apple strudel wherever I go.

The bus stop is at the end of the block and takes only 10 minutes to get into the center of town. From there, I can get another bus to Salzburg, which is only about one-half hour away. Even though it's January and I'm in the Alps, I came prepared with thermal underwear, furry boots, a hat, and a long fur coat. The cold isn't bothering me at all.

Salzburg is gorgeous and so rich in culture with its baroque architecture and beautiful palaces. It is also the birthplace of Mozart and the setting for the film *The Sound of Music,* both made obvious everywhere. It's so enticing that I take a *Sound of Music* day tour to visit all the sites it was filmed except for the opening number on top of the mountain that cannot be accessed in January. To my surprise, the tour is great fun, and with the tour guide's CD of *The Sound of Music* playing the whole ride, the small busload of people, including myself, sing every song.

On the weekend, I take a train to Vienna. When I arrive at the hotel, I feel the reception is rather cold. But I must be imaging it. Maybe not. When I ask for recommendations around the immediate area, it's as if I'm asking them to personally escort me. I get nowhere except a point of the finger in the direction. Direction of what? It's dark out now, and the snow is really coming down. It's incredibly beautiful. I continue walking "in the direction" for some time and hope to find a place to get a bite to eat. The buildings are magnificent: large, white, and at night there are white lights all lit up on most of them. It's Christmastime in January, but on a bigger scale, a much bigger scale. I am so taken with everything around me that between the beauty of the buildings and the falling snow, I don't even see what's immediately in front of me until I'm almost on top of it. There's only one other person around, and the gentleman explains to me that I am standing in back of the palace. BACK of the palace!? I quickly ask how to get to the front, and he tells me to walk through the archway. Walking from one end of the passageway to the other, there are shops along the way and horse drawn carriages passing through, and I feel like I'm in 1800 or I just walked into another movie. As I come out of the passageway, I see to my right the expansive white Parliament building down the street all lit up and then turn to my left to see the front of the palace. I'm so floored by its beauty, my body jerks back. The second floor windows nearly the height of the room have their chandeliers lit with women in gowns and men in tuxedos dancing below them. I feel like I am five years old and I just received my first jewelry box. I open it, and the ballerina is dancing. With the snow falling heavily, my breath is taken away.

On the weekend, I board a train for Budapest for two nights. Once again, I'm lost with my geography and think I'm traveling west. Luckily, I meet two incredibly sweet Rumanian sisters on the train, and the time passes quickly. We make plans to meet up the following morning for them to show me the city. Once we leave the station in Budapest, I sense something is different from any other place I've been in Europe. I can't put my finger on it; something is different, and not for the better.

At the hotel, all I need to do is walk up the stairs to the reception, and before saying one word, the clerk knows I'm American. How could this be possible? What is giving it away? It's such a large hotel, could I be the only one they are expecting tonight? Doesn't seem possible. I'm given a room immediately next to the elevator the size of a bathroom. This is what the inexpensive rate gets you. The noise of the elevator door opening and closing keeps me up all night. I'm too tired to get up and complain, and if I insist on changing rooms, I'll end up paying more. So, I stay.

The following day, my new Rumanian friends and I hop on a bus. There's a young lady with an older woman sitting in front of me. Their seats are facing the side of the bus, whereas I'm facing the front, and I can see everything they do. The older woman is probably her grandmother, as she sits next to her holding her hand, never letting go. It is the sweetest touch, the feel of unconditional love, of comfort, of family. I think about my own grandmother, and I feel the tears begin to well up inside me; I miss her terribly. As I leave, it finally dawns on me what has been so different about this place after all. Part of it was the gloomy look of the city, the quiet in the dark, but what pierces my soul is their expressionless faces. No one smiles. Life is apparently very difficult for so many of them here. I am happy they have each other.

I came to Budapest really to experience their world renowned fabric-free thermal baths, and I've treated myself to a massage. I have no interest in going to a spa nude, but as it turns out, I have no bathing suit, and being it is January, I can't find one to buy either. I thought that when in Rome - or Budapest - do as they do; that is why I am here anyway. It's something entirely different, entirely European. So before my massage appointment, I walk into the immense and gorgeous thermal bath with its domed ceiling, columns encircling it, just to look before going back to swim or soak in this amazing place. I've never seen anything like this; not even in a movie. It looks like I've stepped into old Pompeii. But when I look at the women, most of them nude, I just cannot get beyond this; I can't even look. As quickly as I entered the baths, I leave. As it turns out, I'm not European at all.

It's getting near the end of my trip; it's almost February and time to go home and face the music. Once I know how much I need to pay for Dad's home, I immediately need to put my house on the market, get a mortgage, AND get a job. All major undertakings. I thought this past year with the two trips to Italy and all the riding would help me mentally, but I am still stressed knowing what's needed to be done. And what kind of job will I get? I don't want to go back into an office, but my degree is in business. Commissioned sales is too stressful; you never know from week to week what kind of income you'll receive. And no one makes good money going into a new field for quite some time. I don't have time. All I know so far is that I'm not selling Dad's home to anyone other than myself. God will have to figure it out and let me know. I pray for answers.

It is my last day in Germany, and my friends take me to the church in Berchtesgaden where they were married many years ago. She tells me that this particular site is the most copied Christmas scene in the world. The churches in this area are like those I saw in Austria, dripping with chandeliers, just like the church in *The Sound of Music.* From there, we go to the Berchtesgaden National Park. It's all so beautiful in such a small area, all in the same town. I have my Nikon around my neck, and once again I'm faced with God's stunning beauty surrounding me. Just yesterday we saw people taking a large sleigh ride through the woods. This is magical..........................until it's not.

I can't stop pointing and shooting my camera; one more gorgeous sight after another. The three of us walk further into the woods just above the border of the lake to get a great shot. We don't go 200 feet, and the conversation again turns to the Americans. He's gone as far as telling me the United States government knew that Pearl Harbor would be attacked on that December morning and did nothing - because our government didn't care! Now he's gone much too far. I cannot get away from these people fast enough. They can stick their strudel up their ass!

I tell them I never heard anything so ridiculous in my life. You're still buying that Nazi propaganda? I'm more enraged because my dad was a WWII vet. I know what the U.S. and Allied Forces did for Europe. I know the Americans lost nearly half a million men and women alone. Where would HE be if not for these soldiers? You hate us so much that you'd never visit America, but not so much as you didn't stop your own son from being educated there? Thank the good Lord I'm leaving tomorrow!

When they drop me off, I am very polite and thank them for their hospitality, but they can tell it's not the same; they've gone too far, much too far. She asks me to email her when I arrive in the United States to know I returned safely.

***

I email my German "friend" only after I get one from her and thank her, but I never write again. I cry for the next six weeks. I had never felt such hatred from complete strangers. I cried for my dad, an American soldier. I cried for all the soldiers that gave their lives for these ungrateful people. I cried for their families!

Shortly after returning home, I met with my doctor, and when I told him what I've experienced in Germany, I heard for the first time that this is where the Nazi movement started. I had no idea, and now I see that the hatred of the Americans over the decades just procreated. How did I end up in Nazi heaven?

On September 2nd, I closed on Dad's home and paid the full appraised value, not one dime of a discount! When Dad's assets were distributed to the three of us, it would turn out that we received nearly exactly what Dad had written to Rose in her dream!

My own home sold in one day, but not without more debacles getting my tenants to leave. I continued with the temp jobs and working part-time evenings until a permanent position became available six months later.

Angela moved out of the basement and purchased a home with her new boyfriend, and cousin Joe moved back into the basement.

In memory of my father, I began volunteering at the Veterans Memorial Home once a week assisting a senior with playing Bingo, accompanying them to a dinner and dancing, or spending the day pushing them around in their wheelchairs for an outing in Atlantic City at the casino. I felt almost as if I was doing it for my own father. It was an honor being of some service to them!

Eight weeks after the closing, I was going through the stacks of mail on my kitchen table. Now with the war of the siblings behind me, I could go through my mail without that sick feeling inside. There's so much junk; what a waste of postage! Half of them I don't even bother to open and toss them right into the garbage pile while thinking how my grandparents didn't get this much mail in a lifetime. I tossed the unsolicited letters and flyers without even a glance except for one. It's postage was different, not a stamp, and I immediately thought it was junk mail anyway. Taking another look, I see for the first time the name on the return address. All these years later, it's from Preston!!!!

Chapter Nine

Life at home: 2008

*I*n November of 2005, I was stunned to receive a letter from Preston five years after leaving his employment. It read:

"Hi, Debbie. A good friend of mine told me I'd do anything for attention, but I think I was a little over the top with this last shindig!

It's always hard to admit when you're wrong, but as it turned out, I was wrong about a lot of things. I turned the opportunity with you down because I truly wanted my marriage to work, but it was too drugged up, and I couldn't stop it. Of course, my ex-wife nailed me much harder than I thought she would. I didn't give my business the time it needed. My focus was on a quick hit to save my house from my ex-wife, and the rest is history. I do have some good memories, and one of them was my time with you.

My current wife has been no help, but then again, I didn't marry her for her brains. My only reason for this letter is to let you know that I didn't just use you (so to speak), and I went as far as I could at the time. You were smart, good looking, and I admired you. I was happy to hear you went to Italy, and I hope you had a good time.

It took me two years to write to you, and I hope you accept it in the way it is intended.
Wishing you the best,

Sincerely,
Preston"

I couldn't believe my eyes! I came so close to tossing it. I knew he opened his heart. There were no signs of a player either. I also knew how hard it was for him to write this. He had no way of knowing if I'd even respond. Would I laugh; would I think him pathetic? I can only imagine the anticipation he was feeling about receiving my reply. I could have written back and told him to fuck off, but I'd never do that to him given the circumstances. He desperately needed a friend, someone he trusted; he needed me. Unlike the others, I was always straight and honest while everyone else just appeased him. After all, he was paying them or they were living off of him in one way or another. I would often repeat that if he kept these "friends," he'd either end up in jail or in a morgue, and I could tell it wasn't very far off. I couldn't stand to hear about his drug use even if it was recreational. The pot wasn't going to kill him, but the hard stuff would. I'd tell him what a fool he was especially since he had already suffered a heart attack just a few years ago, and I could never understand how his new wife was promoting this lifestyle. It was obvious to me she was more interested in his money. I always walked away in total disgust.

A few days later, I wrote back telling him how surprised I was to hear from him after all these years and that I was sorry to hear of his troubles. I also told him I wondered how many other women he sent a similar letter in the last two years. Lastly, I asked why he waited this long. I ended the letter asking if he wanted me to send him a book, that I would pray for him, and I offered to write a letter to the judge on his behalf. I could speak for the time he was going through the nightmare of losing both his homes to his first wife, and I could attest to his good character I knew well.

I could become his pen pal, but I was very much afraid of getting involved any more than that. I remembered our screaming matches over his dangerous lifestyle and him pleading with me to hug him before walking out of his office. To hug him and walk away was much more difficult than I ever let on.

After six weeks, I made the decision to visit him because I needed to know if after all these years there were any feelings left. I still had not spoken to him, and when I wrote back, I deliberately left out my phone number even though he kept asking. He also kept requesting that I call his daughter, Timi, who would confirm that he's not the same guy and that everyone agrees that this occurrence was an aberration. A week later, I called Timi, and we quickly got into a discussion about Preston's wife and everything I knew, even what she was doing to pay her rent after Preston became arrested. I wasn't going to hold back anything after my last go-around with her father. Timi quickly made it clear that we were in total agreement about her; she would never even take another phone call from her either. I told Timi not to tell her father, but on Christmas morning I was going to visit him.

Preston knew someone was coming, but he didn't know who. He hoped it was me. When he entered and saw me from across the room, he cocked his head to the side and made a beeline for me. My heart started to beat again, and the only thing I felt was fear. What was I getting myself into? He was thinner and older looking, and his once dark skin was now incredibly pale. He grabbed me tightly, but only a short embrace was allowed. I remembered that hug, that hug between two people who care about each other. We sat and talked across a table for an hour, the maximum time allowed, our hands never letting go. As different as it was between us, I still cared. I remembered how kind he was to me and my dad, but I still didn't know how much I wanted to be involved. I didn't want this life for myself either; it was never a consideration, but by the second visit a week later on New

Year's Eve, he was asking me to be in his life more than just a pen pal. I was not interested in any relationship with a married man no matter where he was, and he said he was no longer even responding to her letters. There would definitely be a divorce regardless. Timi was going to disown him had he had anything to do with his second wife after the arrest, and I knew he was never going to let that happen. And what would I tell people? No one who knew me would ever believe I'd get mixed up with someone who was incarcerated. Not in a million years.

On Sunday mornings, I would make the hour drive to visit him and lie to Richard, who was living in my basement again, where I was going. Richard was still never going to be a romantic interest of mine; I just didn't want to hear his comments. From the moment I left my home, I began to feel ill from the stress until I actually saw him. I never knew if there would be a problem and I wouldn't get to see him at all. The waiting to be permitted into the room was the worse. The dress code and guidelines were so strict, they even turned babies away. Would my jean's button make it through the metal detector? What about my underwire bra? If my bra doesn't make it, I don't either. It made me feel as if the guards were treating me almost as if I were a criminal myself. I deplored everything about it. I've stayed so clean my entire life to insure I'd never have to deal with anything like this, and yet I ended up visiting a prison on a regular basis anyway.

Preston said he wrote me a long letter, but I never received it. I started to wonder if he was lying, bullshitting to keep both his wife and me in his life. I questioned him again and continued to wonder if I was being taken for a fool. I started to think if I should just back out and walk away from it all before I got into it any deeper.

Preston believed he would be home in a few years, and I had no way of knowing if he'd return to his old ways either.

197

If he did, the relationship would have been over before it started, and I would have allowed him to break my heart twice. I found it hard to believe he'd do this to me after everything we've been through together, knowing how he respected me, and the attraction we had for one another was undeniable. Still, getting involved with him again could be a huge mistake.

I come home from work, another in-home, commissioned sales position selling food and appliances, and I'm in an especially good mood because I'm meeting Debbie and Jeanne for dinner. The three of us have been celebrating our birthdays for decades, and we know it's always going to be a night of many, many laughs talking about old boyfriends, husbands, and my mom. I don't hear Richard in the basement, and when I reach my kitchen table, I see a note from him. It says: "I've been arrested for back child support." I don't believe my eyes. You've been arrested, too? I feel bad for Richard, but I know his work ethics, and now I see his problem more than ever - alcohol. This is what has ruined his life. I never believed Preston when he'd say that Richard showed up drunk to his office or to an appointment. I thought he was exaggerating, and sometimes I saw he was jealous of Richard being with me. But he was telling the truth. As soon as Richard opened a checking account in town, his address came up in the system, and they grabbed him. Both his kids were already finished with college, but missed child support payments are missed payments regardless. I go to the basement to look for something, and what do I find but Preston's letter - opened! Richard had taken the letter out of my mailbox and read it. Of all the letters I had received from Preston, this was the one letter where he disclosed EVERYTHING we shared between us; not one indiscretion left out. I can only imagine Richard kept the letter because he wanted to reread it - and then reread it again. I can't believe he would do this to me. His jealousy overtook any logic, any decency, and what surprised me the most was that he kept the letter after reading it while living in my own home.

Richard tried several times to call me from the jailhouse, but I never let him get one word in before slamming the phone down. After three attempts, I block the jail's phone number.

Preston has been incarcerated nearly three years, and he's still not sentenced. I've been writing and visiting him on a regular basis for nearly a year now. When I first heard of his problems, I consulted with my monsignor and attorney about the possibility of visiting him because I knew he needed a friend, but they both advised me very quickly to stay away; so, I did. But when Preston's letter arrived, I couldn't turn my back, and when I heard of how things transpired, I understood much more and couldn't blame him. He got involved in something he had no way of escaping once they started to follow his kids and grandchildren. When I told Father Doody and my doctor the full story and about the letter two years after our initial discussion, I was shocked to find they both approved of my relationship with him without hesitation. I never needed their approval, but I wanted their opinions. Actually, no one expressed any real concern at all, not my friends, my aunts, or any cousins I confided in. It was up to me. The only advise Aunt Katie would give me was not to marry him. Jeanne, Rose, and Cousin Cathy would even come to the prison with me to meet him.

The following summer, Preston's divorce became finalized. Shortly thereafter, he was sentenced to 10 years.

It's been three years since I've been on a horse, and I find a riding academy in the Chianti region in the village of Barberino Val D'Elsa right on the main wine route. I print the brochure and show cousin Joey who used to own his own

199

horses and ride with his best friend and cousin Jimmy San Filippo, an older cousin of ours. Joey's and my grandmother was born a San Filippo, so Joey and I are of San Filippo blood. The stables were a hangout for Joey and Jimmy. Sometimes they even bordered the horses in Staten Island and rode along the beach. It was a great life for city boys!

Jimmy and the horses have been gone for quite some time, and Joey misses his best friend and cousin terribly. When I show Joey the photos of the riding academy, to my utter disbelief he wants to go, and I couldn't be happier. Riding in Tuscany with my cousins is a dream come true. Joey, his wife Jackie, and I are going to Barberino!

***

The three of us land in Rome, and we make the three and a half hour drive to Casa Frassi in the heart of Chianti. I made reservations for two nights to relax before our riding begins and for my cousins to experience my favorite vineyard. Excited and positive, I know how to get there off of A1, but I miss our exit and lose the experience of taking them up the most scenic route of all, Chianti's famous wine route. When we finally reach our destination, they, too, are impressed driving up the long, cypress lined driveway as we wind through the dirt road to the stately main villa that draws you in from nearly a half mile away. As a returning guest, I request two rooms with the best views in the pinkish stone building where breakfast is served. To me, the definition of happiness is opening your shutters in Tuscany for the very first time and seeing the amazing landscape. I'm really happy today, and so are they.

It's our first day, and we drive to Siena, my favorite Tuscan city. I know exactly where to park so we won't have to walk up any steep hills. When we reach Piazza del Campo, it's time for lunch outdoors in Siena's most famous piazza. Here we just linger and people watch just like the Italian do. The same mime is there right in front of our restaurant just 10 feet away wearing the same old suit jacket and same old beret that must have been his grandfather's. He is funny, though. He performs for the people eating in the piazza by surprising the passersby with his antics. He sees an older couple walking together, and the husband's head is turned away from his wife looking at the buildings as he's passing them. The mime gets between the two and grabs the husband's hand. He thinks it's his wife's hand he's holding. The look on his face when he discovers it's a complete stranger (and a man, too) is priceless. People are always caught off guard, and it's always funny.

201

After two days at Casa Frassi, we head north to Barberino to the riding academy. Driving in between the rolling hills, vibrant red poppies appear in abundance alongside meadows of wild flowers in shades of yellow and purple. When we arrive, to our utter disbelief, we discover that the village the riding center is actually located in is San Filippo, and not Barberino. The three of us believe it was either Cousin Jimmy or our grandmother in heaven, or both, that had their hands in this. What were the odds we'd be riding in San Filippo and we'd be with family? This is so perfect!

The stone farmhouse built in the late 18th century has two levels and an additional central turret. It is surrounded by hills, woods, vineyards and olive groves and has a 360 degree panorama. Flowers are in full bloom all around the property, and red geraniums in large planters sit outside the main door. The window frames are faded red with intricate lace curtains that cover the glass, quintessential Tuscan.

There are two apartments, one inside the main residence on the main floor, and the other, a detached unit that I reserved. The detached one gives us more room, privacy, and a patio that none of the others have. Except for the other apartment, the remainder of the guests have just a bedroom off of the dining room. Everyone eats dinner together, typically about 25 people from the United States and Europe, and whatever the cook made that day is served family style. There isn't a bad dinner here. People come and go throughout the week, and there's never a dull moment.

Our detached apartment is adorable. It is actually built into the side of the mountain just feet away from the main house. There are two entrances; one on the upper level with a door that's only about 4 feet high, and to reach the other door, you walk around the stone structure and down the 12 steps shaped into a half moon, a spiral staircase built into the side of the mountain, to reach the sliding glass door in front. There's a working kitchen on the left, an old wooden table for four, and two single beds in the back corner with a small bathroom under the stairs that leads to the loft. The loft is where my bed is and is where I can also enter through the small door. It's perfect for our needs. Sometimes one of the cats finds his way in and will sleep next to me on top of my carry-on. Joey tells me something I had never even considered: our apartment was originally a stable. How appropriate!

In the morning after my shower, I put my makeup on at the kitchen table while sipping cappuccino. Joey and Jackie have been up for some time, and Joey's already been to the dining room for breakfast. We don't care for the Tuscan breakfast with their heavy cakes, cheeses, yogurt, or their cereals with too much chocolate in them. And their bread is so hard I'd be giving it to the birds if I were home. By the second morning, Joey finesses the cook bearing a strong resemblance to Gina Lollobrigida to make eggs for him every day.

We quickly discover that they don't canter at all when they go into the fields. I can't believe this is happening again! I made the assumption we would be cantering given it's an academy. I'm so wrong. But Joey doesn't mind that the horse is not going faster than a walk; he loves riding in this breathtaking landscape.

I'm so upset that I won't be cantering after coming all this way with my cousins, I take lessons most days instead and befriend my trainer, Cath, from New Zealand. After dinner, she mentions she has no means of transportation to the house where the owners have a room for her. She's not even given a bicycle. The home is near the entrance to the road coming into the center, and it must be near a half mile away. It's so dark, you cannot see your hand in front of you, so I ride her home after dinner whenever she dines with the guests. As I'm driving her home on the winding, dark, narrow gravel track, she points out a hole in an old tree. She tells me there is energy coming from it that draws you into it; it's not sinister, just heavy, she says. She continues to tell me that one day as she was passing downhill she looked back at the old stump and saw the spirit of a little boy sitting there. She asked him what he wanted, but he only smiled; she thinks he just wanted the recognition. Cath further explains that the location of the riding center is situated as a stopping point for the trip from Rome to Florence and how she can just imagine the amount of deaths that occurred here either by accident or murder. She's not afraid though; they are friendly ghosts. You can't see your hand in front of you, but she sees a ghost and is not afraid. I'm afraid just riding past even in the daylight.

This academy is a place where most people come to learn dressage, another important fact I missed! Joey and I are not dressage people, so we don't ride with them and normally are only with the others at dinner or when we see each other in the stables. On our last day, I decide to skip the ride and get a massage at a nearby resort while Joey and a few others are riding out to go wine tasting at a local winery. I'm not a big lover of wine, or really any spirit, but there is something about having a glass or two of wine and then getting back in the saddle. If Joey could, he'd change the itinerary and do this every day - preferably for the rest of his life.

After a week of riding, we head south to Rome. Once again, I'm so anxious to show my cousins around this city, but I receive a call from the agency telling me that the apartment we selected has a problem. There was a storm that blew the shutters open, and all the wood flooring had lifted and can't be walked on now. I'm very disappointed because the location is perfect, it's quiet, something not so easy to find in this city, and the home possesses Italian charm. I don't want to feel like I'm in New Jersey when I'm here. At this late date, I take her recommendation.

We arrive in historic Rome where the first thing we need to do is return our rental car to Termini Station. We nearly kill ourselves driving to arrive on time so we don't have to pay for another day's rental. I tell Joey that the apartment is not far from the station and that the taxi fare should be about 20 Euros. As we're wheeling our luggage to the front of the station, a taxi driver approaches us, and we all get in. With traffic, the ride is under 20 minutes. We reach our apartment and we are immediately across from Castel Sant'Angelo. The three of us get out, the cab driver removes our luggage from the trunk, and then says, "75 Euro." He was clearly taking us for a ride. I tell Joey not to pay him, but Joey doesn't want a confrontation and hands him 75 Euro. I want to call the police because he's a thief, but Joey doesn't want to deal with this today and would rather just pay.

After walking to the Vatican the following morning, we head to the Colosseum, the Roman Forum, The Trevi Fountain, the Pantheon, and the Spanish Steps. Our most popular purchases are for gelato. The following morning we take a sightseeing tour from the hop-on hop-off bus that conveniently leaves us off immediately in front of our apartment. But before we leave Rome, I tell my cousins of an attraction not in the tourists' books just a few blocks from Circus Maximus, an ancient Roman chariot racing stadium. Walking up the hill past the rose garden is Piazza dei Cavalieri di Malta where we find a keyhole in the door of the monastery. Peering through the keyhole, we are able to see that behind the gate is a long dirt path encircled perfectly and exquisitely by evergreen trees that form a canopy, embracing the path and protecting it from the hot Roman sun. At the far end of the path, our eyes clearly see miles across the river for the only view: The Cupola di San Pietro in Vatican City which is perfectly centered through the trees. The view is so unexpected, so stunning, we all get emotional.

Joey's knees are really hurting him, and he's pushing himself to walk. It's our first night here, and the three of us stop for dinner at a nearby restaurant and are seated outdoors. This is the last leg of our trip, and all three of us have already spent more than we wanted, most of it on food and wine and a lot on gas. Joey places the order for us, and the waiter places three dishes of appetizers on our table. Joey tells him that they weren't ordered, but the waiter tells us we'll like them. He says it in a way that the three of us think they are included with the meal - until we get the bill. To have given us one appetizer is one thing, but there's three of them. It's our first night in Rome, and Joey hates it already! Everyone here is robbing us, and he wants to go back to Tuscany. I am so surprised and upset how it turned out, but there's nothing I can do about it. I was so sure he'd love Rome, but it was the Romans themselves that gave him reason to want to be in Tuscany.

I leave my cousins alone to walk back to the apartment, and I go through my ritual of walking over to Piazza Navona before returning home to bed. I'm so excited; it's been three years, and I can't wait to see what kind of performers and exhibits are there tonight. The excitement and energy of Navona will make Joey happy to be in Rome; maybe tomorrow night he'll feel better. This magical, ancient ground possesses power by its mere existence. It's stunning beauty captivates you, and there is no place more magnificent in Rome at night than dining in this amazing piazza. As I enter from one of the side entrances, I cannot believe my eyes. More than half the people are missing, the entertainers, the vendors and the patrons, and it hits me smack in the face: the entire world economy is struggling, not just America. My heart sinks.

***

After returning home, all three of us, Joey, Jackie, and myself lost our jobs due to the recession. I started a master's degree program just six months before the layoff, and I made the decision to continue with the degree and pay for it myself. By the time I finish in 18 months, the prediction was the economy would certainly turn around, I'd get a better job, and I'd have the student loan paid off in three years. That was the original plan.

Many months after returning home, I receive two traffic violations amounting to more than $300 from the Italian authorities for driving in a bus lane the day we returned our car to Rome. All because I was trying to save a day's rental.

It would take two years before I could forgive Richard for stealing my letter from Preston. I started to again invite him for dinner on a regular basis. I hated what he did, but I forgave him for one reason: he was good to my father when it mattered the most!

Preston was moved to another state, and instead of visiting him once a week, my visits became less than once a year.

Chapter Ten

Life at Home: 2010

I'm still unemployed and finishing my master's degree in accounting. I start to think about my old friend Linda, the same Linda I met in Rome in 1970. I thought of her often over the years and how I admired her courage. She endured such a difficult childhood with her dad walking out on them, her mom passing shortly thereafter, then raised by a wicked grandmother, that I had a soft spot for her. So did everyone in my family. Mom nicknamed her Silly Putty, a description Linda had for her own grandfather that Mom thought was so funny.

After perusing the Internet, I find someone who may be the Linda I'm looking for, but she has a different last name. I knew Linda had met someone from Florida and dropped out of college just six months before finishing her bachelor's. I couldn't believe it. You're approaching the finish line and then walk away? I had visited her a few times at the university and knew it was difficult for her financially, but with her looks and personality, she had no problem getting jobs that paid well enough to keep her in school. Last I heard she was a Go-Go dancer at the Admiral's Club on the base near the school. She even made her own outfits for dancing. When I hadn't heard from her in some time, I called her sister who told me that she married the guy from Florida suddenly, on a beach or something, and that she wasn't even pregnant. Was I giving her too much credit for being this courageous woman, or was she just an idiot that caused her own problems? I never heard from Linda again.

Through Facebook, I message Linda asking if she had been in Rome in 1970, and I receive a response the same day that it is, in fact, her, now 40 years later! I'm elated I've actually found her after all these decades, and we make plans to speak the following day. She tells me that she now lives in San Francisco and is coming East for her high school reunion. She asks, "Would it be ok to stay with you for a few days?" I immediately respond, "You better believe it! I can't wait to see you."

Linda spends several days with me and makes my life a living hell in the process. She is bossy, pushy, rude, a know-it-all, and a phony, and those are her better qualities. My immaturity at 17 didn't see this, and all that courage was something entirely different, something entirely sinister.

But there's one bright spot in this visit, one very bright spot that allows me to overcome whatever this witch is throwing at me: Linda had a friend whose family is in the movie business, and the woman's parents were personal friends with Frank Sinatra. The same Frank Sinatra whose voice was never further than a button away all those years Dad was ill. The same Sinatra that sang *"That's Life"* that Dad played loudly every Sunday morning, waking us up, until we married and left home. The same Sinatra I would leave long-stem roses at the site of his home in Hoboken, New Jersey, once he passed away. The woman has been deceased some years, but Linda remains friends with her mother and is always invited to join the family in Malibu over Thanksgiving weekend. Linda happily makes the drive from San Francisco to Malibu every year. Just knowing this woman lost her daughter and Linda was her friend, I understand why she'd continue to welcome Linda over the years. That explained the friendship. Linda phones this woman from my home, and the woman invites me to stay at her home after my graduation in Phoenix.   This is **the** best invitation I've ever received <u>in my life</u>! The only drawback - Linda has to take me.

I fly to San Francisco only after Linda has convinced me she is much better now, and the anxiety she displayed while visiting me was due to conflicts with her family.   She convinces me that her bad behavior is behind her, and I accept her excuse because I really want to get to Malibu.   I'm amenable to whatever she wants to do considering I won't have my own car. I'm hoping to see the beautiful Pacific, their magnificent sunsets, and maybe even see a celebrity or two, but I'm really here only as a means to Malibu. As may have been expected, within five minutes of arriving, I am having major reservations, and the trip is to last for 10 days! My return flight home is leaving from Los Angeles, close to Sinatra's friend and eight hours from Linda's home, so I am forced to deal with her alone the first week. But merely two days later, Linda receives a phone call from this woman's granddaughter advising us that she has taken sick and we should not come!   I don't believe what is happening!! I want to scream.

I am suffering through this vacation from hell to get to Malibu and talk about Frank, see photos of him probably never seen before, and now we can't go?   Ironically, the weekend started out with Saturday being the best day of my life. Friday night I flew to Phoenix for my graduation ceremony; I've waited for this pomp and circumstance since 1989 when I was denied any ceremony after completing my bachelor's due to the downpour of rain, thunder, and lightening.   I make this trip because this graduate degree has been one of the most difficult things I ever accomplished.   Twelve accounting courses, twelve A's.   I'm proud of myself, but I'm concerned about the big student loan I now have and the job market. It's not at all what Obama had promised when I started this program. We are worse off than ever in the job market. Once again, I'm in a position where I'll accept any reasonable job. Not at all what I paid for at the age of 57!

The closest I had to family attending my graduation was Aunt Dee watching the ceremony live on the computer. She saw me receive my diploma and hear Condoleezza Rice's commencement address. After an electric ceremony, we celebrated with a beautiful luncheon my counselor, Heather, arranged for us at an historic restaurant in Phoenix. An unbelievably good day! But then I make the crucial mistake of flying to San Francisco the following morning. I went from heaven to hell overnight. A precipitous fall, to say the least. The visit proved she's not only bossy, pushy, rude, a know-it-all, and a phony, but she's the biggest freeloader I've ever met. I'm mortified to be associated with her. I'd walk through hell for Frank, but this is too hot.

Thank God for Linda's friend Bobby, an acquaintance she scammed into picking me up at the airport, who sees my desperation and offers me some marijuana. She is so offensive that I call Jeanne everyday and instruct her what to do should I go missing or found dead. This is a vacation from beautiful downtown HELL!

Luckily, I do get to drive down the famous crooked street in San Francisco and dine at their wharf thanks to Bobby, an unexpected life saver for me this week. With him, we enjoy a gorgeous walk via a footpath directly to the beach and watch the fireworks on the 4th of July at the Sausalito Pier with some of Linda's acquaintances. But then Linda goes too far when she blasts Bobby and me in a restaurant because she "sensed" we wanted to be alone. Bobby becomes enraged and storms out. I just stand there, watch, and wonder how this is going to play out. Bobby has driven us here, so as infuriated as he is, he's driving us back home. I want to get as far away from this beast as possible and think about asking Bobby if he would take me home with him for the next few days until my plane leaves, but I don't feel as though I know him well enough to ask that much of him. He told me he wanted to spend time alone with me, but days? I am too embarrassed to ask. Mistake!

The whole experience shocks me. I thought I was a pretty good judge of character even when I was young, but I had overlooked things in 1970. I come to remember being embarrassed when she was unkind and rude to a woman in our Italian group. But I was a minor in a foreign country, and I knew no one other than the people in my group whom I had just met. I very much welcomed her friendship.

I notice a difference in both women and men who weren't raised by their own mothers. There seems to be a disconnect, a void. Linda lost her mom very young. Would she have been a nicer person had she been raised by her, I don't know. I find her qualities offensive, to say the least. Compared to Preston's childhood where his dad passed when he was just 10, put in a boys' home at the age of 15 and remained there until he became emancipated at 18, Preston could not be any more different; there's no one less offensive.

My best friend Jeanne and I have a saying: "We go in search of people, and our problem becomes......... WE FIND THEM!" No truer words were ever spoken.

***

In 2010, I return to Italy and revisit my favorites places: Maria's farm, Acquaviva, near Cortona, and then go riding with Jenny for a few days.

It's terrific seeing Maria again, and I finally get to practice speaking Italian. I love it, I love the family, I love living on a farm for a short time, and I love her cooking, everything from pizza to Steak Florentine. The weather is

212

beautiful, and during the day I can leave the door open and have just the heavy, thick ropes hanging in the doorway to keep the flies from entering. The neighborhood dogs stop by to check me out, as they pierce their shoots through the ropes. There's three of them, all stopped at the first step into the apartment. The German Shepherd is the bravest; he comes right in. One of the horses decides he, too, wants to check me out and pierces his nose through the ropes. He actually picks his one leg up to enter the apartment, and I leap forward to back him out.

I drive to Cortona and find a beautiful sunflower plant for only three Euro for the apartment. It's perfect for the kitchen table until the following morning when I find a trail of ants and put the plant outside my front door. As I go to turn back into the apartment, I see the horse coming to me again. This time I run in and close the door. When I eventually emerge, I see he chewed the sunflower head off the plant and just left it on the ground for me to see. At dinner that evening, I tell Maria the funny story, and she couldn't believe it. The following night I enter the restaurant and have the only table with fresh flowers. That's my friend Maria!

Jenny has only two guests riding this week, a young Indian girl from the U.K., a freelance writer, and me. The girl is very lovely, and when the three of us are together hiking, the conversation turns to politics. I'm not an expert, but I understand money, and I'm not happy with what our new president is doing regarding healthcare. For the last decade, I've been paying my own health insurance and managed without any public assistance. It never even crossed my mind. I'm not afraid to say I don't agree with the fact he was throwing it down our throats and being voted on without even having a chance to read it. I ask them: "Who signs legal documents without reading them?" Apparently Congress and the Senate do. Jenny turns to me and says, "I think he's too good for you Americans." I don't think Jenny thought at that moment that her comment would be so offensive that this would be the last time she would get my business. Sounds more like another American hater to me.

In 2011, I began to work as a tax intern for a small CPA firm and finally secured a position worthy of my education. To my surprise, I was good at it; actually, very good, and I liked the work. Within three months, I catapulted myself into a position I would never have dreamed possible in such a short period of time, especially at the age of 57. It would normally take years at any age. But it all came to a sudden end when I became upset with the owner. As was his normal course of action, he told me not to return. My undiplomatic mouth has once again hurt me. I knew I was right, but I lost the battle anyway.

In December 2011, I received devastating news that my niece was diagnosed with breast cancer; the same young niece with two small children that lost her husband exactly one year to the day from a heart attack. I hadn't spoken with either of my siblings or their kids in 14 years, and all of a sudden the hatred, the anger, and all the resentment I felt so intensely for all those years was gone, and all I could think about was everyone's pain, their suffering. I sent my sister and her daughter a card with a note telling them how deeply sorry I was for their pain, and a few days later the same niece invited me for Christmas. After 14 years, the families reunited, and nothing was ever said about the past. It's been buried. All we care about is my niece.

Preston always said he was going to bring my family back together. I could never see that happening and never knew why it was important to him when it hadn't even been a consideration to me, but just months before he comes home, my family reunites. Life changed in a moment. The youngest sister and I will never be friends, but we can at least be in the same room without attorneys being present and have a conversation. It's a major improvement.

On January 30, 2012, eight and a half years after being arrested, Preston is released from prison and moves in to my home just two weeks after I started a new job. Other than my father, I have not lived with another man in 33 years, and suddenly Preston and I are tied to each other for his six-month home confinement period. In my heart, I know the mere fact that we have to live together for some time gives our relationship a better chance of survival. We'll have to make it work. He's been telling me for years that on his first night home he just wants me to hold him while he cries all night long and rid the pent-up feelings he's been dealing with for nearly a decade. The hardest thing for him to accept is losing all his assets and having nothing left to leave his kids. I remind him what a great dad he was to them growing up and that his ex-wife, who was granted his money, would leave it to his kids anyway. I remind him he has his life, his kids, and a future, a happy one at that, and that my life is moving forward, in the direction of Italy, and ask him where he wants to be, stuck in the past and crying over his mistakes, or does he want to join me? His blues quickly fade.

I didn't know if I could even undress in front of him now. So many years have passed, and we're quite a bit older than we were all those years ago when our passions for each other ran so high. But right from the start, he'd curl into me like a pretzel at night. It became about affection and attention more than anything else. He always thanks me for waiting for him all those years, not knowing how truly compatible we would be. He knows one thing for certain: I'm not like either of his wives, and if I ever thought there was an indiscretion, the relationship would be over the same day. My logic says that he is over this bad stage of his life for a number of reasons, and one of them, his age. Overnight his life changed from being locked up in a prison to his biggest concern being where to store all of his matzoh.

The laughs come so easily for both of us. Some nights I get into bed and start a comedy routine about how my electronics hate me. I tell him that it has gotten so bad that when I put an address into my GPS, it told me "there is no fucking way I'm taking you there!" I was making it up as I went along. It was hysterical, and the laughing felt like it went on for hours. In the mornings, he awakens me very gently with a backrub and butterfly kisses and then packs my breakfast to take to work while I shower. I knew for years that he hated cats, but I didn't know if I'd fall out of love with him if he didn't like my Nia. This could be the deal breaker. But she'd change that herself, and he falls in love with her every morning when she greets him at the bedroom door the moment he opens it. Like he's talking to a baby, he coos, "Hi, Nia; hiiiii." He's almost singing it. He bends down and grabs her tail, and while still holding onto it, they both go into the kitchen where she'll direct him right to her dish while she very impatiently waits for him to fill it up. We watch GMA together while I get ready, and we have a routine going just like any other family in the world. The only difference is he legally can't leave the house. From work, I can come home for lunch, and every day when I walk through the door at 12:45, lunch is on the table. What surprises me the most is our closeness. Holding me at night in bed, he says, "When I go, tell people about us." He is always so amazed how two seniors could find such happiness at this stage of our lives. This kind of happiness and contentment is a new experience for both of us.

But we still have our major differences. The most difficult is how I feel about the people he welcomes into his life, the same logic we fought over all those years ago. Even though I can control who walks through my front door, I can't let go of this "disconnect," as I see it. He never sees evil in people even when it stares him in the face. I would repeat what my mother taught me how I would be judged by the company I keep, but he has a tremendous amount of pride in the fact he can mingle with anyone from the janitor to the CEO.

Just before returning home, Preston met a young man, and he's very fond of him. Preston would tell me how handsome and nice he is. I ask what he is incarcerated for, and Preston says "bank robbery." My mind is screaming, oh, yeah, a real nice fellow. Of course, it was a one-time occurrence and he's straight now.......... until we hear of another bank robbery on the local news where he was caught. It was actually his third bank robbery that day! He got caught when the taxi driver who was driving him to the different banks became suspicious and called the police! We don't talk about how nice he is anymore.

To Preston, everyone is a nice guy; they are just people like himself who made a big mistake. He believes their stories, their version of the crime. Preston's lost somewhere between childhood, manhood, and the hood. But my fears of him wanting anything to do with his former life and wife go unfounded. The only other women he wants in his life now are his daughters. He'd have no better place to be than standing next to me anywhere I am in the world. He feels safe.

Other than his low standards on friends, Preston and I rarely have any problems getting along, and I enjoy the company of someone I am really compatible with. When our differences are so vast about people and their behavior, I tell him that I'm going to call his daughter, Timi, and ask her what she thinks. He knows she'll agree with me and gives up. It would be worse than calling his mom. He adores Timi.

Once the six-month home confinement period is over, I introduce him to my entire family. My friends are fond of him, and they're always happy to be in his company, but I have no idea how my family will respond knowing the circumstances. In a short time, though, they accept and genuinely like him. Several of my male cousins do, however, come forward and warn him about being good to me, just in case.

Preston craves my attention and affection so much so that it's like having another full-time job. On Friday nights after work, we make chocolate martinis and dance around the kitchen while I cook, and on Sundays, we play Dad's old Frank Sinatra albums and dance on Mom's tile floors while the gravy is cooking. And several days a week while I'm working, he juices and drives it over to my niece's home several towns away in the hopes it helps with her chemo. He even volunteers for my church, knowing it will make me happy. Life is getting better and better, and my only real concern in life is my sister and her kids. Things have certainly changed!

I receive a phone call from my cousin Joe who has rented my basement apartment off and on over the years that he has lost his job due to the recession, and now he is having a problem with an addiction to pills. It has gotten so bad, he is placed in a mental institution. He calls begging me to take him out of the institution and live in my basement again. Within weeks of Preston's home confinement ending, I have two men living in my home. Sadly, the very next day Nia is found dead from old age. Life again changed overnight.

Not surprising at all, Preston really enjoys my cousin's company, but after a short time, my cousin begins to bring riff raff around. When he gets out of hand, he's not allowed back into the apartment. Shortly thereafter, his sister needs a place to live when she lost her job, and I have her move in the space her brother just left. Suddenly, it's as if I'm running a motel. I'm happy to help my cousins!

On January 30, 2013, one year to the day Preston moved in, I'm in surgery for breast cancer. Unlike both of my nieces, I only need to have a lump removed and go for radiation. No chemo. I am certainly happy not to have to go through the suffering they do, the absolute suffering! but I feel so guilty. I have no children; why couldn't they have been the lucky ones and caught it early? I cannot rejoice at all!

Because my sister has been involved with breast cancer and her daughters' choices of doctors, I already have a network to go to because of her. It saves me the tremendous burden of finding and selecting doctors for something so serious. She attends my doctors' appointments with Preston and me. She knows far more than I do on this.

I've been telling Preston for years that when he returns home we'd sponsor another child through Children International in addition to the boy I already help. We talk about it many times with me telling him to check the website and select a child - any child. A letter arrives from Children International asking for help with a specific child. Reading it, I notice the boy has the same birthday as Preston AND the child was born on the very same day I purchased my father's home, the same home I nearly killed myself to keep and then purchase.   We took our new boy, and luck came back to me that very same week.

On April 27, 2013, we become engaged.

***

It's 2013, and I can't believe Preston is actually coming to Italy with me. My heart races as we go through security, as if we are doing something wrong, but the new passport and the letter from his parole officer in my pocketbook say otherwise. I know we got help from the heaven's above because getting approval to go before his probation ended turned out to be an error by his parole officer. When she realized what she had done and tells him that he cannot go, he doesn't get upset and tells her that he'd stay home but they'd have to reimburse me for the non-refundable ticket I purchased for him based on what she's already signed. I was beyond upset, but Preston never lost his temper even for a moment with her. That is his temperament, and he knew getting upset with her would never help.

An hour later, his parole officer receives final approval for him to accompany me. I assume she didn't want to have to deal with the fact that she had signed the one-page request without even glancing at it. What were the odds she'd make this mistake and then have to live with it? Winning the lottery seemed more realistic.

Our first stop is Acquaviva for three days where Preston would finally meet Maria and her family that I've been talking about for years and experience himself firsthand her cooking and hospitality. Preston is surprised and a little nervous how easily I take the turns climbing the mountain to the farm with our 4-cylinder stick shift. After all this time, I am driving them nearly as quickly as the Italians. When we arrive at the farm, no one is around, and when I look at the front door of the apartment I always rent, the key is in the door. We walk in, and there's a fire going in the fireplace just waiting for us. That's my friend Maria!

221

Just like me, Preston falls in love with the family immediately. He can't believe how Maria greets me, yelling, "Debbie, Debbie, Debbie!" like I'm a long lost relative. I am stunned and very happy to hear that her life has become much, much easier. Her restaurant became more successful than she ever imagined, so much so that they no longer have pigs or sheep, AND she has retired from teaching.

After three nights, we reach our riding center in the stunning Val D'Elsa region of Tuscany. This particular riding tour is given only twice a year, so I'm very surprised when there are only two other women joining me, two female acquaintances from Colorado. I'm also surprised and very happy that they haven't canceled the tour with just three people, another sign that the world economy is still struggling. Preston will easily keep himself entertained until we arrive back from our ride each day. There's always someone around at a center to talk to, plus he has his iPad, a Wi-Fi connection, and an exercise room. He's never lonely.

The rides are glorious cantering besides such vineyards as San Felice and La Selva. I've never seen such beauty even in the movies. Here we ride down dirt roads lined with cypresses over 80' high, and I'm in my glory. But the owners don't like the way I've been taught to canter where I lean forward and hold onto the horse's neck, and they disallow riding this way. Now, I'm instructed to lean back when cantering, more like a galloping position, and it's so much more frightening because I have nothing to hold onto except the reins. I'm flying without a net, so to speak. If I pull too hard on the reins, I could make it worse. Then, for the very first time, I'm instructed to ride immediately behind the owner. I can't believe my ears because only the better riders go behind the guide. My heart is racing as we take our first canter down this magnificent cypress lined road when the handsome

owner looks back at me and yells: "Breathe, Debbie, Breathe."
My breath is literally taken away. I didn't dream this big!

For the first three days, we are given a different horse
each morning to determine which one we are most compatible
with. On the fourth day, I am given a horse that doesn't like to
walk; he trots regardless of what the others are doing. After
five or six hours of the constant jolting, I suffer a back injury.
Incredibly, though, the only time I feel any pain is when I lay
down. I'm forced, however, to give up nearly all of the
remainder of the rides that week. Instead, Preston and I visit
different villages and hamlets each day, go for spa treatments,
and spend a day at the thermal baths in Rapolano Terme. Each
evening we return home before dinnertime to a feast at the
center with the other riders.

In Rome, we have a great, small apartment merely two blocks
from the Pantheon on the third floor facing a piazza with a
high-end restaurant that is always packed with motorcycles
and cars double and triple parked. The bedroom is centrally
located in the apartment and has no windows, so noise is
never a problem. We feel like real Romans, especially when
we go food shopping. If I just hand the cashier my Euros and
never speak a word, they'd never know I'm not Roman.
Preston is getting to have the same feelings.

Life at Home: 2015

On June 16, 2015, the day before turning 62, I retire. The decision was made a year ago when my employer told me I had to remove the words "Be Blessed Today" from my email signature. The Chinese had complained to him because it was religious. It was more than I could tolerate, and I had to leave the very first moment possible.

Family and closest friends are invited to celebrate my retirement with an antipasto and ravioli dinner in the yard, my first birthday party since turning 17 in 1970, just three days before leaving for Italy the very first time. I cook everything myself and start months earlier. I hire an Italian singer for the occasion, and everyone gets to see my newly renovated home for the first time. Over 50 cousins will anxiously come this Wednesday night; they will come for my ravioli!

The day after the party, Preston and I plan to drive to Florida and stay with my beloved cousin Junie whom I haven't seen in over 20 years. Junie and I lived in the same house as young kids, and the only thing separating us was a staircase. To me, she wasn't only my cousin, she was my big sister and my best friend. Then, when she was 11 and I was 8, they moved away, and we rarely saw the family. The laughter in the house was suddenly gone, too. It was horrible, and the emptiness, the missing, never faded away. Mom became pregnant shortly afterwards, which gave us reason to be happy in the house again, but I missed my cousin; always did; always will.

Junie's sons are giving her a birthday party for her 65th the weekend after I turn 62. I tell her that Preston and I will drive down to attend her party. We'd finally get to celebrate our birthdays together again after all these years, all these decades! Her mom's birthday was June 16th, mine, the 17, and hers, the 18th. Even after all this time, we'd always think of each other on those dates. Now Preston and I plan to drive the 1500 miles to make it just in time for her party.

Preston picks me up on my last day of work so he, too, could say good-bye to the ladies I work with. He doesn't know them well, but he knows how hard they work and how they are treated by the owners. As a man who operated his own business before being arrested, Preston always had a heart for his employees and treated everyone like friends. Both Preston and my employer are Jewish, but they couldn't be any more different. This man doesn't even buy us water, and in the winter, we are forced to wear our coats and scarves at our desks because he's too cheap to heat the place properly. It's sad leaving my coworkers behind, working so damn hard and me not being there to help them anymore. It's bitter-sweet saying good-bye. As an accounts receivable manager, I have gotten to know many customers and have a very nice relationship with nearly all of them. The only time they speak to me is when I am asking for money. So, when I called a customer to say good-bye, he actually says, "I love you, Debbie." I am so moved - so emotional; we have never even met.

As we pull into the driveway, Preston asks me to enter the house from the front door because he wants to show me something. He says he has a gift for me, something that will help with my party. I don't want to take away the excitement of his surprise from him, so I just follow his directions. He says it's in the basement and that he wants to video tape me walking down the stairs to get my reaction. I follow him down the staircase slowly, with skepticism, and when I make the turn on the bottom step, for the first time in over 20 years - Junie is there!

There was never a party for her. She didn't even remember why she made up that story. She was probably afraid I'd ask her to fly up for my party and didn't want to ruin the surprise and didn't want to say no either. But she hid Preston's plan to get her to attend my retirement party for two months, and by the time she arrives, she is so frazzled from all the lies she was telling me. When I would ask her about her party plans, she'd make things up. I even bought a new dress and had it tailored for her pretend party. Preston never once tried to stop me from packing or shopping for anything that had to do with her fake party, and I never once thought I wasn't going to Florida.

It is, by far, the greatest surprise of my life, and there would never be a better day in my life to do it - the day I walk away from work forever! I never suspected a thing. The electricity, the excitement began the moment I walked through my front door. I can't contain my excitement, and I start to jump for joy like a child. Preston knows how happy he made me; he is doing everything he can to thank me for all the years I waited. We are both elated.

The atmosphere of the entire party the next day is nothing short of electric, and it is like a dream when I also get to surprise my sister and Aunt Dee with Junie. I don't ever remember such joy like this, such happiness with my family, something we all need. Everyone came to eat ravioli, be with their cousins and listen to Italian music. Preston hosts the event and does a very funny skit performing as an "Italian." He loves Italians, their culture, and, of course, their food, but he also loves being Jewish.

After the shock of seeing cousin Junie, I sat down to write my speech. I thought about the different careers I had over the last 45 years and how they shaped my life. But I knew what my family wanted to know, and that was the truth about Preston from me. So, I take this opportunity to set the record straight:

"...........Over the last 44 years, I have had different careers. About 20 years were spent in outside sales dominated by men. One year after my father took ill, I was forced to find another job. It couldn't be an office job because of my dad's needs. I walked into an interview one day and was hired for yet another outside sales position working evenings. A few weeks after I started, I met the very nice and very handsome owner. In a short period of time, I saw the difference between him and all the other salesman I had ever worked with. He was kind to everyone, the employees and the customers! But he was also kind to my dad. Over the four years I worked for him, I got to know him well, and we enjoyed each other's company. At the end of the fourth year, I saw trouble brewing and left his employment. We never spoke again. I heard of his troubles through a mutual friend, and knowing his character - and his heart - it killed me. I spoke with my priest and lawyer, and they both advised to stay away. So I did. But nearly five years later a letter arrived from him. This time I wouldn't turn my back....

Obviously, we are talking about Preston. After living alone for three decades except for eight years with my dad, I was very concerned about what it would be like living with him, especially considering he was much wilder than I needed in my life! My faith has paid off........He has not only made my life fun for the first time, but he has given me my family, something money cannot buy. I want to thank you for the best birthday surprise I have ever received. To say you shocked me yesterday is an understatement. I not only got a present that lasts for seven days, but so did my family! I didn't dream this big! You are the love of my life, and my friends tell me my mom would approve. So, all thumbs up.

Just six weeks ago, I didn't think tonight was possible. I walked through a door and heard the worst words of my life: "Sit down, Aunt Debbie." But someone above pulled a rabbit out of the hat for my family, and I am so grateful to God tonight. I wanted to really celebrate this occasion; I still can't believe I am living the life I have always wanted - just being home with my guy. Ironically, my mom lost her life at 59 and mine started at 59. And tonight starts the beginning of the best chapter in my life and being with my family and friends.

You never know how life will change when you walk through a door. Here's to never hearing sit down, Aunt Debbie, and here's to La Familgia!

Junie stays with us for a full week, and the only thing that separates us is a staircase, just like when we were kids!

Preston has given me what he promised: a man who is true to me - and he's given me my family back!

***

In September 2015, I begin to fulfill a long-time dream of writing this book from an apartment in the Sienese region of Tuscany set on top of a hill called Montefollonico, a typical isolated Medieval hamlet surrounded by thirteenth-century walls of fired bricks. I wanted a place that was quiet and had a lot of character to inspire me. It had to be in a village, and it had to be behind the medieval walls. I wanted authentic; I wanted to be a villager. The apartment was originally a wine cellar, so it's unique in itself. We also have a private backyard with a beautiful view of Montepulciano. Other than a big villa, nothing screams Tuscany more. I fell in love with it at first sight, and this is where I've come to write over the next six weeks.

We both love the apartment, and the only time we fight is when Preston forgets to close the heat valves. I keep telling him how expensive heat is here and that we will be charged for it according to our contract. He can't believe I pay for heat separately, but I keep telling him that's it's typical for an entire apartment. For the first two weeks, I don't want him to turn it on at all. When it becomes cold to the bone, I put the oven on and open its door, and we're comfortable within minutes.

The oddest thing in the apartment is the layout of the unit where you cannot go into another room without climbing stairs. There are three steps going down into the living room from the front door, three steps down to the next landing, one step up to the bathroom, six steps down to the bedroom, and then three down and five up to the kitchen, and lastly, three up to the backyard. All steps are made of stone, of course. I worry one of us will fall in the middle of the night going to the bathroom.

The television stations are all Italian or Arabic with the exception of only five English speaking channels that include a replay of Jimmy Fallon (not a full show) and a BBC channel. The amount of Arabic channels is alarming to me. I never noticed this before in Italy. So, after a few days of trying to find an English channel, we stop trying. Preston is more than interested in watching the Hillary Clinton Benghazi investigation, and luckily we are able to view it live on the computer. When we get into our oversized bed, we watch YouTube acts, normally comedians, sometimes for hours. Besides writing nearly two chapters a week on my own book, I read three other books the first two weeks with having no television. Preston is always connected to the news via the Internet and obsessed with what is going on with ISIS and our lack of leadership. I don't blame him. It frightens me tremendously, and there doesn't seem to be anything we could do about it. I pray for our country, for Israel. Our lives became so different now in nearly every way.

Dressing for bed, I see something on the bedroom wall and think it is possibly a decoration. It looks like a small lobster, but it definitely doesn't go with the Tuscan decor. Preston checks it out, and to our disbelief, it's a bug! It's actually frightening; we can't believe how big Italy grows their insects! Who'd expect they'd grow their bugs like they grow their lemons, jumbo sized. Preston says their moths alone are the size of birds. Every night before getting into bed he makes an insect inspection throughout the house. We don't think too much of it, but later on we find out that the lobsters were actually scorpions!

It seemed in the beginning of our visit that we'd have a problem with something in the apartment every day. The shower wasn't working properly, and the water kept changing from very hot to very cold without touching the faucet. When we put the oven on for the first time, it blew out all the electricity in the kitchen. They had to remove the entire oven and return it the next day to repair it. And the light bulbs keep burning out. The owner is very good and fixes everything immediately, but I'm embarrassed with all the lights burning out. She'd certainly think we were inconsiderate and leave them on all the time. That isn't the case at all.

When it rains, we just stay in, and I write while Preston keeps himself busy by visiting his new friend, Umberto, that owns *Hotel La Chiusa Ristorante*, the nicest restaurant/hotel in town, or keeping in contact with the outside world via Facebook and emails. In between my writing, I cook. In the local grocery store, we find a jarred Bolognese sauce that I could not make any better myself, and it brings me back to 1970 and what the monks served us that I enjoyed so much.

Our part of town, the medieval part, has only two main streets. We are at the end of one, and there's everything except a post office on the block: two high-end restaurants, a grocery store, two churches, a bank, and a pharmacy. Everyone we pass on the street is friendly and says "*Buon Giorno*" or "*Buon Sera*" to us. Except for the three restaurants and cafe immediately outside of the wall, the town rolls up their carpet early. The street lamps lit up at night on our cobblestone *strada* make it look more like a postcard than a place we actually live, albeit only for six weeks.

On the days we have beautiful weather, I stop writing and we go village hopping. I can never get enough of the landscape, and when we see all the villages written about in the surrounding area, I look at my paper map and pick a route designated as the most scenic to ride that day. We never know where it will take us, and it doesn't matter. One day we inadvertently walk right into a movie set for the filming of

231

"*Medici*" starring Dustin Hoffman. We are in God's magnificent playground just hanging out, and it is all good!

For five mornings in a row, I awaken and yell out, "Mom." My mom passed in 1988, and now all of a sudden I'm calling out for her automatically the very moment I awaken. I have to believe she is with us, nothing else makes sense to me, and having heard that spirits use up energy, I knew her presence had to be the reason the light bulbs keep burning out. But Mom never had any interest in going to Italy, and I'm curious how long she is going to stay. Over the next few days, I've come to believe Dad is here, too.

Preston can't believe how it feels to be here in Italy for such a long time. This isn't merely a vacation; it's a sojourn, and he is beginning to feel assimilated and loving it. An afternoon driving to the big supermarket, the COOP in Sinalunga, is something we both love doing. We can't believe the size of their cheese department or all the wines and liquors they sell as if it were bottled water. When we select an item in the fruit/produce section, we weigh it ourselves and generate a price tag. If we need a large shopping cart, we have to pay one Euro just for the rental. There are also small, red plastic carts that you pull around like an old fashioned red wagon that are free to use. We love food shopping days here.

When we leave Montefollonico after our six-week stay, Preston inadvertently takes a bag that belongs to the housecleaner that contains all her cleaning supplies and an attachment to her vacuum cleaner. I don't see it until we arrive at our next destination about two hours away. We notify them immediately that we'll return everything the following Saturday on our way down to Rome.

We drive to the stunning vineyard in the Chianti Classico region called Querceto di Castellina for our next week. Here I know we'll meet up with other guests, and I know there will be distractions that we didn't have in Montefollonico. Preston thrives on meeting new people. It doesn't matter their sex, race, religion, or age. He likes everyone, and this scares me a little. My biggest challenge with him has always been to get him to be more skeptical about people, but that's not who he is. Even his incarceration hasn't changed that. He's still the tall, dark, and handsome guy that loves to joke around with anyone. He simply loves people, and with his good looks and gregarious personality, he never has any difficulty making new friends. I tell him it's a sickness! I've never known him any other way.

The beauty of the vineyard is indescribable, truly majestic. As I open my front door, the vineyards immediately in front of us that cover the land as far as my eyes can see are tilted up as if to greet us, appearing to nearly touch the sky, and I can hear God saying: *"Buon Giorno, Debora."* I reply: "I cannot believe what you created here, Lord." If you don't feel the presence of God here, you never will.

This *agriturismo* has only eight units it rents out, some are attached units, and some are independent. All of them are made of stone with walls four feet thick, and there aren't two that are nearly alike. All of them have authentic Tuscan kitchens and fireplaces. The only updates are to the bathrooms and heating system, exactly where you want them. In our kitchen, there is also a television and a couch. Like the house I was raised in, the kitchen is the heart of the home. Other than sleeping, life is here.

A few nights after we arrive, we hear a loud commotion coming from the main building immediately next to us. There's two American couples sitting on the veranda right next to the tall gas lanterns. They're drinking wine, laughing very loudly, and playing cards. As I'm crossing their path to get to the washing machines, we acknowledge each other and say hello. I continue to go back and forth to the machines, and after a while, they invite us to join them. They're two attractive couples, one from Alabama and one from Florida. It is terrific to see couples get along so well and see this much happiness and laughter. They are old enough to be my much younger siblings and young enough to be Preston's kids, so I didn't think they'd be interested in spending time with us and were just being polite. But despite our age differences, we spend each night together until they leave for home, laughing, drinking and playing cards into the early morning hours outside on the veranda just steps away from our front door.

The week is filled with more village hopping and driving up long, cypress lined driveways to see what's at the other end. It never gets boring. In the beginning, Preston kept his iPad open on his lap and would play chess while I drove. After some time, though, he, too, was taken by the exceptional beauty of the landscape and put the iPad down. And to my surprise, he is never getting bored with looking at new and different villages either. I've got a guy that loves Italy, too!

We take day excursions to Florence and just window shop the famous jewelry stores on the Ponte Vecchio and then walk to the San Lorenzo Market to get great Christmas gifts of leather bags and even a coat from the designer for my sister. I take photos of different pocketbooks and send them to cousin Junie to pick one out for herself. Because the prices are soft, Preston has the job of negotiating, and he's enjoying it. In the end, he never fights me about any decision, and we are both happy with the amounts he settles on.

Before we leave Chianti Classico, I take Preston to the Florence American Cemetery and Memorial where nearly 4,400 Americans are buried liberating Italy during WWII. It started with one incredible mission: Operation Mincemeat.

With the approval of the Allied Forces, the British's deception plan, saved Europe. It was accomplished by persuading the Germans that they had, by accident, intercepted "top secret" documents. The documents were attached to a corpse deliberately left to wash up on a beach in Punta Umbria, Spain. As a result of this misinformation, this scam, the Nazi's relocated 90,000 soldiers to Greece, an entire panzer division, with their equipment and thereby would lose Sicily. The Allied Forces suffered great losses in Sicily's invasion alone: 5,532 men killed in action, 2,869 missing in action, and 14,410 wounded. Italy would lose 4,678 men killed in action, 152,933 missing or prisoners of war, and 32,500 wounded.

This was the beginning of the end for the Nazi's, but it would take yet another two years to get from Canada's first airdrop of men until the Allied Forces reached the top of Italy and finally get to destroy Mussolini and Hitler. By the end of 1945, the U.S. Military, Army and Navy, launched Operation Magic Carpet and Operation Santa Claus to process the thousands of GI's for discharge in time for Christmas. It has been called "the greatest celebration in American history."

Even after all these decades, it's so emotional, and when you see the headstones just lined up, the <u>thousands</u> of them, lined up all the way to the top of the memorial, you are immediately affected by their loss, by the loss of their families! What everyone gave up to free Europe - all because of one sick Nazi!

From Querceto di Castellina, we are driving to Rome for our final week where I booked an apartment just feet away from the Pantheon. Before returning the rental car, we need to drop off our luggage at the new apartment. But first we must return the cleaning supplies to Montefollonico. Two hours later we meet with our former house cleaner, and what does she have in her hands but more new light bulbs. I guess my parents stayed a while longer after all!

Over the years, I've come to really appreciate how I plan my own trips, and I definitely like making Rome my last stop. From here, we will walk Via del Corso from Piazza Venezia all the way up to Piazza del Popolo and many of the side streets in between where I will do all my shopping and stop at The Spanish Steps and the Trevi Fountain in between. Moderately priced shops stand alongside the high-end stores. There is so much; I never know where to look first. From our apartment, we are equal distance to the Coliseum as we are to the Vatican. At night, we can walk to Trastevere, Piazza Navona, Campo de' Fiori, and for the first time visit Rome's historic Jewish district. But before leaving the city, I will climb The Holy Stairs on my knees (the only way allowed) and pray for my niece.

The roads in Rome are not built on a grid like New York City, and so many of the streets in historic Rome are really just for pedestrians. Locating a building on an ancient, narrow, cobblestone road just feet away from a major attraction like The Pantheon is really only done by people that are very familiar with the city's roads. I know how to get around but only on foot. I know the apartment is central to everything I want to visit, and I can get to them within a 30-minute walk. But we need to drop off the luggage first. It becomes apparent soon after arriving in historic Rome that the GPS cannot get us to our apartment because it doesn't recognize that so many of the roads are only for pedestrians, and after some time, I let Preston leave the car while I stay with everything in a packed piazza. If a cop comes by and forces me to move, I don't have any idea how I'll find Preston. Our phones only work when connected to Wi-Fi, and we aren't connected while on the road. Some time passes with no sign of Preston, and I believe he lost his way back to the car. Fortunately, he found the apartment and got help from the owner getting to the street. From now on, I'll spend the extra 65 Euro, return the car to the airport, and take a taxi with the luggage from there.

On our last day in Rome, we walk to Campo de' Fiori to their open market to look for some great deals and quickly find them. When I go to pay the vendor for the merchandise, he inadvertently returns the same 20 Euro bill I handed him in addition to the change. I immediately hand it back to him and explain what he did. He thanks me, and we walk away. But Preston asks why I gave it back and said that the vendor wouldn't have returned it to me. I tell him it isn't my money and that it is the same as stealing. I tell him if we had kept it, this kismet would come back to us at some point. That's how the universe works.

The very next morning we leave our Rome apartment to board a plane for home, and Preston realizes he forgot his I-Phone at the apartment. He had been so sure it was packed in his luggage, but by the time we arrive in Canada to catch our connecting flight, I receive a text from the owner telling me I left an I-phone behind. It would cost me to mail it back, but we'd get it back! The universe did, in fact, come through.

***

Two months after arriving home, Preston and I drove from New Jersey to Florida via Alabama to visit cousins Junie and Joey and our new friends we met on the vineyard. Our new friend, Christine, would offer help and provide me with invaluable input for this book. God sent me an angel via Alabama. Who knew?

On Sunday mornings, Preston and I still play Dad's old Frank Sinatra albums and dance on Mom's tile floors while the gravy is cooking. If we're in Italy, we do it on someone else's tile flooring. And that all-night cry session.................. he never needed it; he's been too happy. Any tears he shed were always from laughter.

LIFE - WHAT A BEAUTIFUL CHOICE!

Winter 2017:

Preston and I rescue a Ragdoll cat. We have been wanting another cat after our beloved Nia passed a few years ago. We drive over an hour away to pick her up, and we know we are very lucky to have been chosen to adopt her from a very loving school teacher who hated giving her up.

The following day, a young, newlywed couple arrived who were staying downstairs for a couple of weeks. I am with the woman alone while doing laundry, and she tells me they're expecting and how excited they both are.

I go upstairs, and Preston is playing with our new cat, Ivanka, who is with us for all of one day. I say to Preston,

"She's pregnant." Preston looks at me with a much surprised look on his face and asks,

"How do you know?"

"How do you think I know?" In a joking, sarcastic tone, I say, "I didn't do a urine test on her. She told me; how else would I know?"

Preston, still looking puzzled, replies, "When did you find out?" "How did it happen; she just arrived?"

Dumbfounded, I look at him and can only say, "WHAT?"

He replies, "Don't you think she should have told us before?"

Still dumbfounded, I say, "How is it any of our business?"

Looking at me, he says, "Are you going to return her?"

"Return her? To who? Who do you think I'm talking about?"

EPILOGUE

After all the trips to Italy over the last 45 years, this is what I've learned:

- Never cross the Alps without a sweater - and a best friend
- There's nothing like riding through the vineyards on horseback - nothing
- Italy became the Italy we know today in 1861
- Even the old changes
- The Italian pastime is walking
- Reunions don't always turn out well and sometimes they are better than ever imagined
- Helicopter riding & hot air ballooning are very cool!
- Italian women work really hard
- Yes, your young daughter needs a chaperone
- People are not always what they seem
- I never want a car with a manual choke again
- Be aware of bats when swimming
- When I go to the graves, they hear me
- My parents and grandparents still visit me
- Italian hospitals have better food than the United States
- I'll always love to canter
- Sharing an experience with someone you love more than doubles the pleasure
- Romans do think they still run the world
- Do the right thing and you will be rewarded
- I love to speak the little Italian I know
- I'm an American first, then an Italian
- God has blessed me
- The Pieta' is still my favorite piece of art

- Some roosters are nocturnal
- Finding family is amazing - It's the friends you may want to skip!
- Italians enjoy life more than we do; they don't have the same financial burdens we saddle ourselves with
- Three-month vacations should be taken after any loss
- My father beat me to Navona
- When a very handsome young man is standing in front of you on New Year's Eve - kiss him!
- There's no feeling in the world like arriving into town on horseback!
- Italian Americans use more ricotta and mozzarella cheese than Italians do
- Italian bread is tasteless - until dipped in olive oil
- Wine is cheaper than water in Italy
- Italians enjoy sipping espresso standing up
- The Italians greet you with a kiss on both cheeks - even the MEN!
- If one child learned what Christianity is all about from those 8 1/2 years of service, it was worth it.
- Always follow the Lord
- Music soothes the beast
- Always call home

What I've Learned in Life:

- Dancing to Frank Sinatra singing loudly is terrific on any continent. If the gravy is cooking, it only enhances the joy
- The most important relationships you can have are with God and your parents
- My mouth is my blessing and my curse
- Hatred is taught
- Common sense is more valuable than any education
- The most important things in life are free
- ALL caregivers need to be watched with a Baby Cam
- The first teaching in Christianity is to help those less fortunate
- There's no force greater than love
- You know you've done a good job raising your kids when everyone is laughing at the kitchen table
- Try to live by the 10 Commandments; they're the only laws we really need
- La famiglia e' tutto, the family is everything
- At the end of the day, always pray for your family and their families, and when you can't pray for your enemies, pray for their children

Postscript

- Linda continued to try and call me, but I refused to answer her calls or her emails.
- Richard never came around again once Preston moved in. Sadly, he eventually ended up in a nursing home.
- When Cesare was told that Preston would be joining me, he was no longer interested in meeting me. He never answered a subsequent email, and we never communicated again.
- Rose is still my second mother
- My niece, Desi, remarried, and her condition has improved.
- My sister and her husband suffer greatly as a result of their daughter's illness. My relationship with her is loving but remains fragile and at times contentious.
- The youngest sister and I rarely see each other, but we remain polite on those occasions.
- Cousin Junie and I will never be separated again and speak all the time.
- Aunt Dee and I are close again.
- At the end of the day, it's my sisters I pray for.
- Jeanne is still single and would welcome husband #4.
- Debbie tragically lost her only son suddenly on January 1, 2016. Her husband suffered a major stroke 10 months prior and remains in rehab. On Sunday afternoons, Jeanne and I visit Debbie at his rehab center.

Thank you for taking the time to share my story with you! I would love to hear from you. Please visit Facebook.com/MyLoveAffairWithItaly to leave any comments and to view photos from each trip.